OX3/03-7/06

Uniforms

Books by Paul Fussell

Theory of Prosody in Eighteenth-Century England

Poetic Meter and Poetic Form

*The Rhetorical World of Augustan Humanism:
Ethics and Imagery from Swift to Burke*

Samuel Johnson and the Life of Writing

The Great War and Modern Memory

Abroad: British Literary Traveling Between the Wars

The Boy Scout Handbook and Other Observations

Class: A Guide Through the American Status System

Thank God for the Atom Bomb and Other Essays

Wartime: Understanding and Behavior in the Second World War

BAD: or, The Dumbing of America

The Anti-Egotist: Kingsley Amis, Man of Letters

Doing Battle: The Making of a Skeptic

Uniforms: Why We Are What We Wear

Editor

English Augustan Poetry

The Ordeal of Alfred M. Hale

Siegfried Sassoon's Long Journey

The Norton Book of Travel

The Norton Book of Modern War

Coeditor

Eighteenth-Century English Literature

☆ UNIFORMS

Why We Are
What We Wear

PAUL FUSSELL

Houghton Mifflin Company

BOSTON NEW YORK

2002

For information about permission to reproduce selections
from this book, write Permissions, Houghton Mifflin Company,
215 Park Avenue South, New York, New York 10003.

Visit our Web site: www.houghtonmifflinbooks.com.

Library of Congress Cataloging-in-Publication Data
is available.
ISBN 0-618-06746-9

Printed in the United States of America

Book design by Victoria Hartman

QUM 10 9 8 7 6 5 4 3 2 1

The author is grateful for permission to quote from the following works:
"Gloria," from *The Poems of Lincoln Kirstein,* by Lincoln Kirstein.
Copyright © 1987 by Lincoln Kirstein. Reprinted with the permission of
Scribner, an imprint of Simon & Schuster Adult Publishing Group.
From a View to a Death, by Anthony Powell. Copyright © by Anthony
Powell. Reprinted by permission of Heinemann.

To Darling Harriette

Acknowledgments

Five of the people who have helped with this book deserve special celebration. Robert S. Ames, captain, American Airlines (Ret.), has supplied valuable material as well as constant encouragement. London author Michael Barber, of the BBC, seems to know almost everything, and I'm in his debt for his generosity as well as his welcome sense of the absurd. Gwen Gatto has calmly and professionally solved many problems of presentation. Toby Harke, of the Free Library of Philadelphia, has shown herself a model research librarian, wonderfully gifted in tracking down the remote and forgotten. My former student Seth Notes has conducted many interviews with acuteness and understanding. It is not possible to declare my specific indebtedness to these five, but they know the details, and I am deeply grateful.

I also want to thank the following, who have been generous with tips, warnings, clippings, hints, criticism, and much else: Norma Ames, Frances Apt, Nina Auerbach, Mike Bersanti, Karen Behringer, Nancy Behringer, Rocklin Behringer, Mark L. Beveridge, Carla Boyd, Thomas M. Butler, Chris Calhoun, Eric Chinski, Gayle Christensen, Elinor Cowhig, Mary Ellen Creamer, William Deadwyler, Tom Downes, Jonas Fang, Betty Carol Floyd, Joan Forman, Sam Fussell, Jim Garman, Lise Gibson, Sir Martin Gilbert, Rabbi Levi Haskelevich, Lynn Henson, Loretta Lawrence Keane, Kevin von Klause, Charles Krzciuk,

John Lappe, Charles F. Main, Sister Margaret MacDonell, Dotti Martin, David McCullough, Father Pascal Monteleone, Bob Philip, Tiffany Rademan, David Sackarowitz, Agnes Scanlan, John Scanlan, Sister Mary Scullion, Amanda Shiffman, Aaron Short, Mary Anne Smith, Portia Sperr, Roger Spiller, Jill Swiecichowski, Peter Thropp, Tim Vaughan, Christopher Wagner, and Bernice Zucker.

And if Nelson Quick hadn't generously kept the computer working, there'd be no book at all. Bless him.

Contents

Uniforms

A Thing About Uniforms

"Society, which the more I think of it astonishes me the more, is founded upon cloth." Thus Thomas Carlyle in 1836. Little less astonishing today are some of the cloth objects chosen by their wearers. But when such objects become, like uniforms, obligatory and regulated, with implications of mass value, they are irresistibly fascinating.

ALL MY LIFE I have had a thing about uniforms. Although it would be pleasant to assert that as a newborn I noted that all the boys were lapped in little blue blankets, with the girls uniformly in pink, I wouldn't go back that far. But it is undeniable that as I aged I began to appear in a sailor suit (this was in the late 1920s), complete, despite the short pants, with whistle and lanyard and red sleeve insignia featuring eagles and chevrons.

Next, my loving mother went into action to accouter me as an ideal Boy Scout, with the result that at troop gatherings I was conspicuously overdressed among boys who as a sophisticated gesture wore only a part of the uniform, if that, at a time. I had the whole thing, and brand-new, comprising breeches, long socks, Smoky Bear hat, official shirt, neckerchief, even official shoes. The rest of the troop appeared in blue jeans or corduroys, with perhaps a neckerchief fastened by a rubber band. (Mine was secured by a costly official slide.) The whole thing was a terrible mistake, resulting in my deep humiliation and rapid resignation from the Boy Scouts. This was all highly ironic, for, entirely uninterested in Scouting "activities," my reason for joining was actually the uniform alone. And also not to be forgotten was the invariable Sunday uniform for church-going, consisting of dark suit, white shirt, black shoes, and understated dark tie.

This was at the time I was in high school, and attracted to the Junior ROTC, but only because those enrolled in it performed their evolutions in full dress uniform and, sweating profusely, were excused from showering afterward. (I had a horror of exposing my babyish body.)

The ROTC uniform consisted of olive-drab trousers and wool shirt with black tie, the whole gloriously completed by a real U.S. Army jacket, but with bright blue lapels to distinguish it from the jacket worn by real grown-up soldiers. There was plenty of brass to convey a military look, lots of buttons and lapel ornaments in the form of discs exhibiting lighted torches (of "learning"). Keeping these, as well as the brass belt buckle, shiny was our prime military duty. There was never any other homework.

Later, at college, I proceeded to join the Senior ROTC (Infantry), which meant furnishing myself at government expense with a real officer's uniform of the 1940s, including pink trousers and greenish-brown jacket. But still distinguished from actuality and seriousness by the shaming letters ROTC on the cap badge and the lapel brass US's.

General Colin L. Powell (U.S.A., Ret.) has testified about the way uniforms first attracted him. When he was a student at New York's City College, "during the first semester at CCNY, something had caught my eye — young guys on campus in uniform." As soon as he could, Powell joined up, and he was not alone. "CCNY was not West Point, but during the fifties it had the largest voluntary ROTC contingent in America, fifteen hundred cadets at the height of the Korean War.

"There came a day when I stood in line in the drill hall to be issued olive-drab pants and jacket, brown shirt, brown tie, brown shoes, a belt with a brass buckle, and an overseas cap. As soon as I got home, I put the uniform on and looked in the mirror. I liked what I saw."

So did I on similar occasions. But fantasy suffered a cruel deflation in the terrible hot summer of 1943, when I had to trade my pseudo-officer's gauds for a real private's baggy fatigues for basic training at Camp Roberts, California. If one ever achieved a pass there, one sweated in enlisted men's khakis while drinking beer and eating steak off the post. When I moved on to the Infantry School at Fort Benning, Georgia, the daily uniform changed to light green cotton overalls and helmet liners. These remained the fatigue uniforms when, commissioned, I joined an actual infantry division.

Shipped to France, we wore uniforms still, but in combat we removed all shiny insignia, secretly pleased to imagine that, as identifiable officers, we were the special targets of German snipers.

The point of all this is that, until mustered out of the Army in 1947, I lived in a constant environment of uniforms and in the atmosphere of the human uniformity they were designed to produce. The tradition continued during my many years as a college professor, where practically compulsory was the daily get-up of gray flannel trousers and tweed jacket, often, of course, with leather elbow patches, suggestive at once of two honorable conditions: poverty and learning. In *The Professor of Desire* Philip Roth saw to it that his alter ego, David Kepesh, says to his students, "However you may choose to attire yourselves — in the get-up of garage mechanic, panhandler, tearoom gypsy, or cattle rustler — I still prefer to appear before you to teach wearing a jacket and a tie." The distinction Roth makes is really between uniforms and costumes.

It is a distinction not always easy to make, but still some principles hold. Uniforms ask to be taken seriously, with suggestions of probity and virtue (clergy and nuns, judges when robed), expertise (naval officers, senior chefs, airline pilots), trustworthiness (Boy and Girl Scouts, letter carriers, delivery men and women), courage (U.S. Marines, police officers, firefighters), obedience (high school and university marching bands, Ku Klux Klan), extraordinary cleanliness and sanitation (vendors of ice cream on the streets, operating-room personnel, beauty salon employees, food workers visible to the public, and, in hospitals, all wearers of white lab coats, where a single blood stain might cause shame and even dismissal). Uniforms also differ from costumes by their explicit assumptions about the way every element must look. Hence the ridicule visited upon Supreme Court Chief Justice William Renquist when, sitting in judgment on President Clinton, adulterer, he chose to appear in a special robe augmented by unprecedented (i.e., "unauthorized") stripes on the sleeves.

On the other hand, ideas of frivolity, temporariness, inauthenticity, and theatricality attend costumes, one reason that Hemingway's Colonel Cantwell, in *Across the River and Into the Trees*, is angered by an Italian upper-class couple who appear to sniff at his uniform. "The pair stared at him with the bad manners of their kind and he saluted, lightly, and said to them in Italian, 'I am sorry that I am in uniform, but it is a uniform, not a costume.'" The colonel is implying also that for an outfit to qualify as a uniform, many others must be wearing the same thing, all more or less conscious of a mysterious bonding by means of — cloth.

But the difference between uniform and costume grows complicated when we consider, say, "cowboys," most of whom turn out to be Marlboro Man impersonators. Their appearance is "uniform," all right — the unique boots, the obligatory jeans, the neckerchief. But as Leslie Fiedler observed in his useful essay, "Montana, or the End of Jean-Jacques Rousseau," what occasioned their uniformity was less their common working experience than the bad cowboy movies they swarmed to on Saturday afternoons. We can infer even from this that when enough people wear the same thing over time, like the dark suits and white shirts of U.S. senators, their costume is likely to ennoble itself into a uniform and convey news of valuable personal qualities in its wearers. And uniforms, even the most modest and apparently demeaning, do tend to ennoble their wearers.

When I first began pursuing this subject, I assumed that many people wearing uniforms in low-paying work resented being the compulsory bearers of such visible evidence of their subordinate condition. But what did I find? All but universal pride in a uniform of any kind, comparable with that felt by an enlisted marine on graduation day. The uniform, no matter how lowly, assures its audience that the wearer *has* a job, one likely not to be merely temporary and one extorting a degree of respect for being associated with a successful enterprise. The uniform attaches one to success.

But what about the outfits far removed from the military or the servants' livery models? What about uniforms more subtly disguised, like the business suit, the dark blue blazer with gray flannel or khaki trousers, not to mention such uniforms as tennis- and beachwear? And what about the recent fad for "casual" dress in business offices, with its delusive suggestion of escaping regulation and unleashing hitherto stifled individualities? It took about a month of the casual fad to reveal that an equally rigid uniform code was now in action, and the obligatory polo shirt came into its own.

Here we encounter a paradox and an embarrassment, which some pages of this book will ventilate. The universal dilemma can be specified succinctly: everyone must wear a uniform, but everyone must deny wearing one, lest one's invaluable personality and unique identity be compromised. If you refuse to dress like others, you will be ridiculed, and no one wants to appear in public dressed like a fool or an oddball. It is not likely that executives will ever skip down Park Avenue at noon wearing tights in fetching colors, and it is equally unlikely that people in general will abandon their secret pride in being identifiably themselves and imagining themselves honored for their originality of appearance.

Unless one chooses to conceal one's physical uniqueness under military or religious garb, there's always going to be an internal conflict between one's aggressive urge to register a singular identity and the opposite impulse, the need to join the crowd and thus risk ridicule, if not contumely.

It's hard to avoid seeing this as a form of madness. Conflicts like this are known in psychiatry to lie at the root of many mental disorders. This conflict we repeat daily as we put on or take off various cloth things with the intention of expressing an identity that will ideally honor our presumed uniqueness. It is a trap impossible to avoid, unless one goes all the way and goes naked. That might be recognized as the ultimate uniform, although it would clearly pose other problems. From the daily sartorial conflict there seems to be no escape — except perhaps to tone down self-consciousness, which is as unlikely as ridding ourselves of the liability to social anxiety.

THIS IS UNASHAMEDLY a book about appearances. I have long despaired of discovering what's really going on in people's insides (like their brains), since the only news available about that is their self-interested testimony. Despairing, I deepened my curiosity about what's happening on their outsides — what can be inferred from their looks, figures, clothing, speech, gestures, and the like. I should also warn you that I have had to restrict myself largely to the twentieth century. My implicit guide has been Erving Goffman's invaluable perception, in *The Presentation of Self in Everyday Life:* "All the world is not, of course, a stage, but the crucial ways in which it isn't are not easy to specify."

This is also a book about the comfort and vanity of belonging, which everyone has experienced. Every soldier knows its pleasures, as does every person who has put on any kind of uniform or black and white formal clothes.

And here I must note and apologize for the unrelenting masculinity of this book. Only recently have women (nuns, nurses, and flight attendants aside) required uniforms (and attempts at their theory), and I have sought to do them justice where appropriate. My experience, on which my labors have largely been based, has installed me inescapably in a man's world, and writing about what I know and have an instinct for has doubtless limited my vision.

I have worn many a trousered uniform and buckled many a cartridge belt, but I have never worn a dress or fastened a garter belt.

Colorful Tights for Men?

After long periods away from England, in 1928 D. H. Lawrence returned to London. The grayness, dullness, and lack of spirit appalled him, and he registered his disgust in an article, "Dull London," in the *Evening News.* While he was away, he observed, a new boring niceness and anonymity had taken over, and all was now tedious and predictable.

A few weeks later, in a further article, he pursued this theme, suggesting the need for a new crusade on behalf of color and excitement as a solution to the dullness problem. Later editors reprinting this piece gave it the title "Red Trousers." "Red Tights" would be better, for that is the sort of garment Lawrence proposed as a replacement for the black or dark gray trousers dominating the male scene. Colorful tights, like those worn by the riders in the annual horse race in Siena, would be a sound antidote:

> It is time we treated life as a joke again, as they did in the really great periods like the Renaissance. Then the young men swaggered down the street with one leg bright red, one leg bright yellow, doublet of puce velvet, and yellow feather in silk cap.
>
> Now that is the line to take. Start with externals, and proceed to internals. . . . If a dozen men would stroll down the Strand and Piccadilly tomorrow, wearing tight scarlet trousers fitting the leg, gay little orange-brown jackets and

bright green hats, then the revolution against dullness that
we need so much would have begun.

The wearers of the red tights, he went on to admit, would have
to be notably courageous, for "it takes a lot of courage to sail
gaily, in brave feathers, right in the teeth of a dreary convention." Needless to say, Lawrence himself never appeared in any
colorful tights, always dressing quite conventionally.

A suggestion of the kind of social punishment awaiting deviation from trouser convention is offered by Stuart and Elizabeth Ewen in their book *Channels of Desire: Mass Images and
the Shaping of American Consciousness*:

> An eighth-grader in 1957 made the mistake of going to
> school one day in a pair of red pants, bought for him by a
> mother unschooled in sartorial logic. As he entered his
> first period math class, his pants caused an immediate
> commotion among classmates. His teacher was so out-
> raged by the transgression . . . that the boy had five points
> immediately subtracted from his average. At midday the
> boy was sent home for causing a disruption. . . . He never
> wore his red pants again.

To make his point Lawrence had to ignore entirely the flagrant colorful details of official and ceremonial London, where
no one could overlook the gorgeous uniforms of the law courts,
the church, ritual politics, and, preeminently, the red-coated
military and the silver-shiny breast-plated horse guards with
plumed helmets. Virginia Woolf invoked these delightfully and
mischievously in her critique of unearned male power in *Three
Guineas*. Addressing an audience of presumably self-satisfied
London males, she presented the view of a highly intelligent
woman:

> Your clothes in the first place make us gape with astonish-
> ment. How many, how splendid, how extremely ornate
> they are — the clothes worn by the educated man in his
> public capacity! Now you dress in violet; a jeweled
> crucifix swings on your breast; now your shoulders are
> covered with lace, now furred with ermine; now slung

with many linked chains set with precious stones. Now you wear wigs on your heads; rows of graduated curls descend to your necks. . . . Sometimes gowns cover your legs; sometimes gaiters. Tabards embroidered with lions and unicorns swing from your shoulders; metal objects cut in star shapes or circles glitter and twinkle upon your breasts. . . . Every button, rosette, and stripe seems to have some symbolic meaning.

But even more striking than the uniforms of the church, the academy, and the civil government are those attaching to the profession of war. "Your finest clothes are those that you wear as soldiers. Since the red and gold, the brass and the feather are discarded upon active service, it is plain that their expensive and not, one might suppose, hygienic splendor is invented partly in order to impress the beholder with the majesty of the military office, partly in order through their vanity to induce young men to become soldiers."

With that last, Lawrence would certainly have agreed, humiliated as he must have been by the resourcefulness and weight of Woolf's rejoinder.

Sturdy Shoulders and Trim Fit

Attention to the shoulders as a theater of honorific male display is standard in military uniforms the world over. As everyone knows, male shoulders, together with chest hair, constitute precious secondary sexual characteristics. It follows that broad and well-developed shoulders are important for male self-respect and pride. Unlike women, whose hips tend to be broader than their shoulders, men's shoulders, ideally, at least, are supposed to be broader than their hips. An infant may ride on a woman's hips, but men like to carry their issue neck-high, spreadeagled on their shoulders. Military emphasis on shoulders thus accentuates the masculinity and presumed bellicosity of uniform wearers. During the Second World War, fashion designers had to go along with the prevailing military imagery and widen the shoulders on women's attire. But, the war over, couturiers quickly reverted to the former "more natural" style. Christian Dior was one who lamented the perversions war had forced upon his garments. It was, he noted, "a period of uniforms, of soldier-women with shoulders like boxers."

Just before the D-day invasion, General Eisenhower was bolstering the morale of the paratroops of the 101st Airborne Division, destined to drop into Normandy before anyone else. Mixing among these anxious troops, Eisenhower started some informal conversations. As was his habit, he asked the men where they were from.

"Pennsylvania," answered one.

Eisenhower noticed the man's broad and rugged shoulders and asked him if he'd got them working in the coal mines.

"Yes, sir!"

Eisenhower, apparently satisfied that this soldier was going to do all right, wished him luck and passed on.

Adolf Hitler was another who regarded conspicuous shoulders as a special index of male strength — and virtue. The perfect physiques of the early SS men accorded with the model for male physical perfection established by the classical scholar and archeologist Johann Joachim Winckelmann in the eighteenth century. Anti-Semitic theory in the German twentieth century came forward to invoke a disgusting antitype, the alleged Jewish male body — unathletic, bookish, ruined by excessive study and attention to the affairs of the countinghouse and the clothing trade. So highly regarded was Winckelmann's model for the ideal male body that his birthday was celebrated in all-male German universities.

Hitler's enthusiasm for this male ideal, available in ancient Greek sculpture, echoed throughout German society as patriotic young men rushed to measure their bodies against the Winckelmann model and the demands of the SS. The object was to assist in generating a "New Man" for the Reich, one strong and brave enough to forward the ultimate transformation of all Europe into something like an immense health farm. The success of the Nazi ideal would manifest itself in shoulder width.

The historian George Mosse, in his book *Images of Man: The Creation of Modern Masculinity,* reprints a patriotic newspaper cartoon of 1933. It depicts Hitler, functioning as a sculptor, in the act of creating this new, physically perfect German. The four panels of this cartoon depict, first, Hitler, together with a bespectacled Jew, viewing a tabletop scene of social disorder, especially street fighting. In the next panel, Hitler smashes this mess with his fist as the Jew looks on in horror. In the third panel, Hitler shapes up a large mass of clay. And in the climactic last scene, he has sculpted a nude statuette of the new male ideal, legs apart, fists clenched, ready for noble action. As the reader leaves this happy sequence he beholds Hitler at his final chore, shaping not the biceps, chest, or stomach muscles but the broad shoulders of the ideal New Man.

IN THE AMERICAN Army from 1918 on, the enlisted men had a grievance not often articulated but deeply felt. While officers could indicate their rank by faux gold or silver pin-on insignia on shoulders, as well as on collar, cap, and lapels, soldiers had to make do with sewed-on cloth chevrons positioned not on the place of honor, the shoulders, but merely halfway down the upper sleeve. One of the revolutionary post–World War II Army uniform changes allows enlisted men to wear their own little brass badges of rank, in the form of chevrons, on collars and shoulders. The effect has been to narrow the visual gap separating officers from men.

Previously, an element of uniform reminding the men that they were in no way like officers was the officer's special shirt, which they were forbidden to wear. It bore shoulder straps, thus calling attention to those sites of honor available only to people of commissioned rank. James Jones, in his novel *Whistle,* expressed the enlisted man's desires as well as anyone ever has. He wanted to depict First Sergeant Mart Winch as thoroughly angry and outraged upon his return to the United States after severe combat in the Pacific. To indicate the nature of his fury, Jones has him locate a tailoring shop in San Francisco that sells him an unauthorized officer's shirt with the significant shoulder straps. Milder versions of this sort of semi-revolutionary behavior were the wearing of forbidden flashy belt buckles and the flaunting of nonregulation jewelry. By the time of the Vietnam War, officers were to be seen wearing shirts without shoulder straps. Now, ironically, such straps performed on only enlisted men's shoulders their original utilitarian function, keeping in place other straps attached to heavy weights carried by the shoulders. And it's worth noticing that in the world of visual fiction — theater, film, and advertising — the locus of the soldier's fictional wound (heroic but not fatal) is most likely to be a shoulder. Today, the popular trench coat is the one with the ostentatious shoulder straps sold by Burberry's. They are quite useless, reduced to the status of a trademark. Without the straps, the garment is merely a raincoat, all romantic suggestion gone.

THOSE WHO HAVE worn military uniform know how it feels when contrasted to civilian clothes. I'm not talking about the glory of full-dress uniform, white gloves and all, but about what is sometimes called "walking-out kit," the way you'd dress leaving the post for the evening or going home on furlough. This uniform usually requires jacket and tie, and it is crucial that the jacket fit snugly, with shoulders emphasized by straps or epaulets and with a crimped-in waist. The trousers must fit closely, with, of course, no pleats, it being a precious military myth that no soldier is even slightly obese and thus in need of such waist camouflage. The shape delineated by the uniform is that of an ideal combatant — athletic, obedient, wonderfully self-controlled, tightly focused, with no looseness or indication of comfort about him. One reason the "lounge suit" was so named on its first appearance is that its looseness promoted lounging, an action unthinkable for a military man. The uniform was made to stand up straight in, and its full meaning is not available when the wearer is sitting down.

The Austrian novelist Hermann Broch meditated on military uniforms as well as on their civilian analogs and arrived at a principle true of both:

> A uniform provides its wearer with a definitive line of demarcation between his person and the world. . . . It is the uniform's true function to manifest and ordain order in the world, to arrest the confusion and flux of life, just as it conceals whatever in the human body is soft and flowing, covering up the soldier's underclothes and skin. . . . Closed up in his hard casing, braced in with straps and belts, he begins to forget his own undergarments and the uncertainty of life.

This military trim-fit look has a history, dating back at least to the eighteenth century, when, as George Mosse pointed out, the image of the man aimed at by the military uniform arose, betraying its origin in the Greek sculptures admired by Winckelmann. The ideal for the contemporary wearer of military uniform was "a smooth body, tight and firm like marble." For the eighteenth century, the opposite image was available in the figure of the effeminate dancing master. If today any item of menswear could be posited as the opposite of the military uniform, it might be the sloppy bathrobe of terry cloth, worn unfastened and in need of laundering.

Thus it was archeological excavation in the eighteenth century that uncovered a masculine form successive ages have taken for granted and allowed to stand as "representative." That is, the new focus on ancient sculpture instructed people in what the male body should look like, or be made by clothing to look like. The ideal male look, wrote Anne Hollander, historian and theorist of clothing, was the one most suggestive of perfect male strength, perfect virtue, and perfect honesty, with overtones of independence and rationality. By the beginning of the nineteenth century, "however a man was really built, his tailor replaced his old short-legged pear-shaped body with a lean well-muscled and very sexy body with long legs."

If it can be said that soldiers are created by their uniforms, what man could contain his vanity when garbed in a suit suggesting a perfect torso as well as immense physical efficiency and ample supplies of courage? Every national defense department all over the world must engage itself in the mental operation of mistaking soldiers for what they have been made to look like.

It is, of course, possible to go too far in the trim-fit direction, as did some Victorian British cavalry units where swank, earned by tightening the uniform, prevented troops from raising their arms to use their sabers.

Russian Uniform Culture

Russia under its last czars," writes the historian Marvin Lyons, "has been compared to a vast military academy." But one signal difference was the wearing of uniforms by people who were not soldiers but highly regarded civilians, like doctors, lawyers, teachers, and pupils at state schools. Karl Baedeker, the publisher of travel guides, visited St. Petersburg in 1914 and testified that "nearly one-tenth of the male population . . . wear some kind of uniform, including not only the numerous military officers, but civil officials, and even students, schoolboys, and others." The court of Nicholas II swarmed with uniform wearers, and even the youngest and tiniest students at the Imperial Ballet School wore dark blue uniforms with collar decorations of silver lyres. So ubiquitous was the uniformity impulse among civilians that aristocrats, bourgeoisie, and laboring classes alike favored quasi-military caps of black or dark blue material with shiny visors.

But it is to the military, naval, and diplomatic services that one must turn to appreciate the unique aspects of Russian uniform culture. Especially notable on Russian uniforms were extralarge shoulder boards proclaiming those two Slavic obsessions, title and rank, by means of colorful stripes and stars of various sizes, and visor caps with outsized covers as big as ashcan lids. The shoulder boards were a favorite target of the

Bolsheviks, who liked to indicate their attitudes and power by tearing the boards off the uniforms of officers they encountered. When they wanted to humiliate the czar upon his arrest in 1917, they stripped off his special, costly sovereign's shoulder boards, which signaled, as they had for generations, the sacred continuity of the autocracy. Nicholas's were adorned with the jeweled initials of his imperial predecessor, Czar Alexander III, just as the czarevitch's were with Nicholas's. He wrote in his diary, "Shall not forget this beastliness."

Shoulder boards were reintroduced by the Soviet army only in the Second World War. When not pursuing their trade in civilian disguise, secret intelligence officers of the NKVD and KGB wore uniforms in public, so powerful was their desire to show off. And so persistent is the popular association of the Russian official look with shoulder boards that the entrepreneurs founding a "Russian" restaurant in New York City were careful to provide their "Cossack" musicians with shoulder boards, together with fancy visor caps with red crowns. Indeed, before the USSR broke up, it retained the czarist sense that officers' uniforms should be extremely impressive, colorful if not gaudy. There's a similarity here to the fanciness of the Soviet subway stations' elegance, with their crystal chandeliers and elaborate ceramic work.

Uniforms worn by those of very high rank, like marshals of the army, consisted of an olive tunic with red piping around the cuffs and collar, collar insignia embroidered in gold bullion, and, on the shoulder boards, an immense single marshal's star. Each trouser leg had a wide red stripe. It was best if the chest, both sides, were covered not just with ribbons but with the whole medals. Marvin Lyons suggests one cause of all this showiness: most army officers were poor, and they tended to originate in remote, drab, unstylish places. "To compensate, perhaps, Russian uniforms had a style and elegance which quite outshone those of foreign armies." Despite the social-equality impulses of the Bolsheviks, this tendency was still visible during the Second World War, and may be taken to suggest acute psychological anxiety about not being valued sufficiently. A useful contrast would be the uniform style of, say, Douglas Mac-Arthur, secure enough in his role to adhere to the understatement principle, wearing that filthy cap with no necktie. And no ribbons or medals.

The German Way

A student of German male clothing in the twentieth century will be struck immediately by the German bent toward national uniqueness. There's not merely the oddity of lederhosen. There's this: during the 1930s, and doubtless before, the public executioner performed his function, by means of an ax, in full evening dress, wearing white tie and tails, with silk top hat and white gloves.

During the Second World War, uniforms were one medium through which German eccentricity most memorably manifested itself. Indeed, writes the uniform historian Brian L. Davis, Germany during the war was "a nation besotted with the wearing of military and paramilitary uniforms of all kinds." And the uniforms and decorations and accessories constituted an immensely complicated special world of meaning and allusion. When highly significant uniform details grow complex, someone has to keep an ultimate eye on things. In Britain that person was King George VI, a uniform pedant if there ever was one. In Germany it was the Führer. When Hitler wanted to punish four Waffen SS divisions for retreating in violation of his orders, he had them stripped of the treasured cuffbands identifying them. That is, he punished their uniforms, which by that time had acquired all but mystical significance. Hitler was especially angry because one of the cuffbands had read *Leibstan-*

darte, designating it the personal guard of Hitler himself, a unit sworn to death before dishonor.

Attention to these German uniforms necessarily drags us into the murky world of twentieth-century German social understanding. Aside from the programs to purify the German race by expelling and exterminating the Others, a key impulse in the social operations of the Third Reich was the urge to uniformity, regarded as the ideal cultural condition. As Joseph Goebbels once said, the object of the cultural departments of the Reich — literary, musical, cinematic — was "to unite all creative persons in a cultural uniformity of the mind." Even on the wartime front lines, the German army emphasized "comradeship" among the troops. One had to be a joiner, and a vigorously enthusiastic one. Ideally, it was thought, comradeship among the soldiers would permeate postwar society as a whole. That is, *Frontgemeinschaft* would bring about *Volksgemeinschaft,* and people of original mind would be recognized as enemies of the state. Doubters, wits, skeptics, ironists, dissenters, and loners would either be quietly absorbed and transformed, or vanish — do not ask where. The Third Reich would finally become one tightly knit whole. The development of handsome uniforms for everyone would provide visible evidence of group cohesiveness and would stimulate citizens' impulses to join in. Far from the unprepossessing olive-drab outfits of the Anglo-Saxons and the Russians, the German uniforms couldn't help appealing to the normal desire of ordinary people to dress up. There was hardly a definable trade or labor community that didn't have its good-looking uniform. To work with your equals, you could dress down in dungarees or protective clothing. But when you wore your walking-out ensemble you could really impress your audience, who would regard you as something special. "Madly theatrical," wrote Kurt Vonnegut of Nazi uniforms, civilian as well as military.

At work in the mines, for example, miners necessarily wore practical, unsightly clothes, but walking out, what a change: an apprentice miner wore a black high-collared tunic with rows of silver buttons on sleeves and chest, twenty-four buttons in all, and, on top, a quasi-military visor cap. As you rose in the mining ranks, your black tunic added silver buttons, to a total of thirty-four. (The German fondness for double-breasted uniform jackets may be explained as a device for exhibiting more buttons.) As a graduate miner, your headgear was a black shako with a large silver eagle on the front and a plume on top. For formal affairs, you added white gloves and a sword and a red-white-and-black Nazi armband. Postal workers and bus and tram conductors closely resembled military personnel, with brass buttons on their tunics and, on their caps, the national emblem — the eagle holding the swastika. A senior locomotive driver got to display on his left thigh a sword in a fancy scabbard with sword knot. Veterans of past wars all had their official uniforms, with aiguillettes, eagles, and armbands.

If you were lucky enough to land a job as district falconry master, you wore a quasi-Tyrolean cap with feathers, to go with your gray uniform, silver buttons, and black leather belt, and since your venue was outdoors, you wore high black boots. Emergency, construction, and transport units had clothing that made them look like soldiers, and were all so attractive that anyone would want to join. An emergency unit commander even got a sword. Workers in the national construction corps were uniformed like troops but with a sleeve band identifying their branch of service. Both male and female members of the German Red Cross were put into uniforms suggesting military connections, with indications of rank on collars and shoulders.

Children were by no means excluded from this national enjoyment of uniforms. Members of the Bund Deutsche Mädel (the compulsory girls' organization) were identified by a black skirt and white blouse. Boys in the Hitler Jugend wore black corduroy shorts, brown shirts with insignia, and black neckerchiefs with leather slide. Leaders could be identified by the junior-sized sword attached to their belts.

Belonging to the diplomatic corps of the Foreign Office did not mean that you were necessarily consigned to a business suit. At formal, white-tie functions, an ambassador wore a black tailcoat with black trousers decorated with a broad silver trouser stripe and, of course, a sword. For walking-out clothes he wore a black tunic with white or silver straps of rank on the shoulders and a silver belt. In cold weather he added a double-breasted overcoat with large fold-back lapels. These critical lapels on overcoats were a standard place to exhibit color as a sign of high rank. A senior Red Cross officer had gray lapels; a general in the engineer corps, pink; a grand admiral in the navy, light blue; field marshal, red; medical officers in the national medical service, brown, like the adults directing the Hitler Jugend. Many military officers wore uniforms requiring breeches and riding boots, highly acceptable because of their association with such former aristocratic activities as animal hunting and steeplechasing.

Another uniform detail unique to the Germans was the semicircular metal breastplate, hanging around the neck by a chain, known as a gorget. Gorgets identified men on military police duty and policemen in general, and suggested an actual armor breastplate. (The troops liked to refer to gorget-wearers as *Kettenhunde,* chained-up dogs.) Whatever their precise meaning, gorgets betokened special authority, and even the supervisor of air-traffic controllers wore one. Their frequent appearance certainly added to the decorative dimension so inseparable from the German uniform practice, like the arm- and cuffbands with words on them, the swords and daggers, and the white skull on the caps of the SS, extra expressive against the customary black background. In the regular army, officers had red stripes down their trouser legs, and even the Gauleiters (political leaders of various districts) got to dress up in quasi-military uniform, with, for verisimilitude, a small pistol in a holster.

But the Navy was one place where some restraint and traditional good sense presided. In fact, the star worn above the gold stripes on officers' cuffs was identical with the one familiar in the American Navy, and the sailors' uniforms were strikingly close to those traditional in other countries. This was a far cry from one of the funniest of all Nazi uniforms, the one worn by the SA (Sturm Abteilung), the original unit of bully-boys in the 1930s who were skilled in beating up Jews, Socialists, and

Communists, breaking windows, and generally raising hell in the interest of the Nazi Party. Having gone too far even for Hitler, they were wiped out by the SS in 1934. The SA wore a sloppy uniform of brown shirt and Sam Browne belt, with brown breeches stuffed into boots. But its most noticeable feature was a little boy's visor cap, a messy sort of soft French kepi with a needless chin strap, always deployed. At this ludicrous little cap no one surely had the courage to laugh out loud, but certainly many felt the urge to giggle, especially when the little cap was worn by the SA's leader, fatty Ernst Röhm. Hitler was once photographed wearing the absurd SA cap, but apparently he was so embarrassed by his appearance that he never allowed the picture to be published. Another photograph depicts him standing with a number of SA people, all in uniform. He is the only one capless.

During the 1930s, such "auxiliary" or political pseudo-military forces were popularly known largely by the color of their uniforms. The SA were the Brown Shirts; Mussolini's private army, Black Shirts. It's hard to think of any military unit on the Allied side proudly known by a color — certainly not the olive drabs of the United States or the khakis of the USSR and Britain.

But the wholly black uniform of the German SS was a triumph of originality, and wearers were so fond of being identified with it that their official periodical was titled *Der Schwarze Korps*. For the SS, blackness could be associated with a whole rich folklore of intimidation and useful wickedness. Listen to Susan Sontag romanticizing Himmler's SS as well as the embrace of black as a sign of power and menace by the lowest sort of motorcyclists. She wrote of these, suggesting a form of sadomasochism, "The color is black, the material is leather, the seduction is beauty, the justification is honesty, the aim is ecstasy, the fantasy is death." A short time ago a new basketball coach at UCLA decided to replace the light-blue-and-gold uniforms of his team with black ones. Complaints immediately poured in, but apparently no complainer dared admit that he was motivated by superstition over the color black — also an obvious occasion of difficulty for "African Americans," once unwittingly stigmatized when called blacks.

Himmler is said to have derived the black SS dress uniform from the black of his admired Jesuits, and since his time black has been associated with all sorts of mysterious evil. In Orwell's *1984*, we become aware of "solid men in black uniforms, with iron-shod boots on their feet and truncheons in their hands." And in Kafka's *Trial*, K. is ordered to wear black during the court proceedings, just as his hostile interrogators do. John Harvey writes, in *Men in Black*, "In Kafka's fiction, black clothing belongs especially to the pursued, accused, judged world of *The Trial*." As the SS discovered, for an interrogator to pry a confession from a prisoner, a black uniform was a priceless accessory.

It may seem astonishing that one German during the war rejected all this gaudiness and blackness. That was the boss, Hitler himself. He needed a "uniform" worn by no one else, and he chose one with an unsuspected taste for understatement. His uniform (it can hardly be called that, for no others appeared in it) consisted of plain black trousers and a light gray double-breasted jacket with only six gold buttons and the national emblem of eagle and swastika on the left sleeve. White shirt always, as if he were a professional, or even a gentleman. Black necktie. No decorations except, from the First World War, a wound badge (he had been badly gassed) and a Nazi Party badge, indicating that he had been in the party from the very beginning. Finally, the Iron Cross First Class, for undoubted heroism. Nothing else. He made much of the symbolism of his gray jacket, swearing that he would wear it until the war was over. He did, although at the end it was bloody and finally burned on his dead body.

His abstemiousness in the matter of uniform was especially notable when he appeared near Hermann Göring, whose fondness for outré uniforms was virtually a trademark, which, combined with his obesity, was a frequent source of silent humor among his audiences. His numerous official posts guaranteed that he had an ample number of uniforms to choose from. He was a general of the infantry, a general in the SS, and a colonel general as commander of the Luftwaffe. His office as hunting master of the Reich enabled him to appear in lots of leather, with a hunting knife in his belt. One of his most pleasing offices was that of general field marshal, for this permitted him to carry a jewel-encrusted baton, which, for his final promotion to reich marshal of the Greater German Empire, he was often able to hold aloft when he was saluted or when greetings were appropriate. These outfits he personally designed, and he was fond of dove gray and, when possible, long coats, presumably to emphasize the vertical when he was rapidly growing horizontal. One of his long fur coats struck an observer as resembling "what a high-grade prostitute wears to the opera." Once, he greeted his guests dressed in a Roman toga and sandals; another time, he sat down to dinner wearing a blue kimono and slippers trimmed with fur. Even Goebbels had a hard time not smiling at Göring's excesses. He writes of one appointment with Göring when he was "received, most charmingly. . . . His dress is somewhat baroque and would, if one did not know him, strike one as somewhat funny. But that's the way he is, and one must put up with his idiosyncrasies." Louis P. Lochner, who translated those sentences from Goebbels's *Diary,* added, "He once received the diplomatic corps dressed like Wotan with an enormous spear." Indeed, he would have been likely to strike later audiences as a sort of heterosexual Liberace, but he vigorously denied rumors that he was addicted to lipstick and rouge.

At the end of the war, captured by Americans, he revealed for one last time his conviction that a person is the uniform he appears in. At this all-important final moment he cast aside these vanities and came forth in what was for him a modest uniform — a pseudo-normal, pseudo-Allied army uniform of his own devising: khaki army jacket and breeches, with black boots. Minimal decorations. Sam Browne belt. White armband signaling status as a mock-humble surrendered soldier. At this moment, he was wearing a soldier's frontline cap. But he couldn't resist carrying at the same time his famous jeweled baton, its glory hidden for the moment in a gaudy cloth tube. He was trying desperately to look as much as possible like a senior officer in an army, and he was outraged to be dealt with as the unique, murderous criminal he was. He was especially angry at being arrested by a mere first lieutenant in the U.S. 36th Infantry Division instead of someone of elevated rank.

One Nazi who, like Hitler himself, avoided all problems of daily uniform selection was Joseph Goebbels, whose outfit was an ordinary double-breasted suit. Near the end of the war, when he was obliged to appear before troops to harangue them toward further heroic sacrifice, he wore an army visor cap and one of those singularly German leather overcoats, but normally, because of his club foot and severe limp, he must have sensed that wearing a military uniform would make him look unnecessarily ridiculous. Everyone knew he had never been in the army, and most knew that his pre-Nazi honors were those of a mere D.Phil in literature, from the University of Heidelberg.

How appalling it must have been to experience the last few months of the war. There was not just the inexorable approach of angry invaders from both east and west and the destruction of the most significant cities by bombing. For a country so wild about uniforms, what a comedown must have been the establishment, in October 1944, of the hopeless ragtag civilian militia called the Volkssturm (People's Troops). It was the yield of the last-ditch mobilization of unhappy males sixteen to sixty years old. These terrified adolescents and creaky old men weren't even vouchsafed pseudo-military uniforms but had to make do by dyeing their remaining civilian clothes army gray or dark brown or by wearing any old uniforms still in civilian hands — antique police outfits, eating club and university fraternity jackets, tram conductors' attire, and attic caches of uniforms once worn during the Great War and the Weimar Republic. Whatever a member of the Volkssturm found to wear, an armband attested to his status as an auxiliary German "soldier." Almost wholly untrained, and equipped with hunting rifles and hand-held antitank rockets, many, as might have been predicted, took the first opportunity to desert or surrender. The more sincere and patriotic were simply blown away by massed

Russian machine-gun or artillery fire. The whole sorry event, which uselessly killed thousands of innocents, would be shocking to normal people, but to Germans, holding high the ideals of uniforms, training, and discipline, it was especially horrible and instructive. The war was ending, and Germany had lost. No more regulated uniforms or fancy dress. As he entered the courtroom at Nuremberg, Albert Speer saw his twenty war-crimes co-defendants for the first time as a group and for the first time brought low. "For years," he wrote, "I had been accustomed to seeing all these defendants in magnificent uniforms, either unapproachable or jovially expansive." What a difference a uniform makes. Now they were simply shabby old men prepared to lie their way out, like tramps brought before a hick magistrate. The self-destruction of Hermann Göring marked irrevocably the death of German dandyism and much else. There may after all be something in Shakespeare's apparent understanding that the fanciest-dressed army always loses.

By contrast, the diarist Victor Klemperer perceived that, the war just over, American soldiers looked hardly like real soldiers at all, their "uniforms" departed so far from European expectations. "They are not soldiers in the Prussian sense at all. They do not wear uniforms, but overalls or overall-like combinations of high trousers and blouse all in gray-green. The steel helmet is worn as comfortably as a hat, pushed forward or back, as it suits them."

Impossible there not to recall Mark Twain's words about a quintessential American: "Huckleberry came and went at his own free will."

Are Italian Men More
Vain than Others?

A *desert in North Africa. January 1941. Sunset.*

> "Do you see that long snakelike procession of men coming very slowly towards us and extending way back to the horizon?
>
> "Who are they and what are they doing?"
>
> "They are Italian officers and high-ranking noncommissioned officers, and they are surrendering."
>
> "What are those loads they're carrying?"
>
> "Those are suitcases, baskets, trunks, footlockers, and garment bags containing dress and parade uniforms, together with appropriate toilet goods and cosmetics. Some appear to be wearing very extravagant headgear, with plumes."

It is quite a spectacle, at once laughable and pitiable, and the memory of it has entertained satirists and their audiences for decades.

The Italian uniform situation differs from the German in several ways. For one thing, some of its features are more retrograde and sentimental, less suggestive of any New Order. Certain uniform items point back to the very early twentieth century and to even the nineteenth. Glory instead of efficiency is the presiding subtext. Consider, for example, the archaism practiced by the regiment called the Bersagliere. Its men wear steel helmets, all right, but attached to each is a large, bouncy bunch of feathers, which may appear as a token of physical vanity, outweighing even threats to life itself.

When Mussolini was young, he delighted in being a member of the Bersagliere. Unlike other units, which marched, it always ran at full tilt, conveying the impression that it was especially military and able. Its headgear in peacetime was a cap with an identifying long horsetail. And in 1926, reports Il Duce's biographer Laura Fermi, Mussolini appeared in a gala uniform "of the highest rank in the militia, bespattered with decorations and wearing a huge white panache [ornamental tuft] on top of his black fezlike cap." In writing about uniformed Italian children under the age of eight, Fermi noted that "the younger the children, the greater was their pride in their uniforms." That may well have been an inadvertent description of all wearers of military uniforms. But there were always what might strike a non-Italian as little slips in taste. When clad in his Fascist black uniform, for example, Mussolini was not above wearing white spats.

Those today in the trade of selling real or imitation military uniforms to "re-enactors" (see "Weirdos," page 126) have some trouble imposing heroic associations on the Italian soldiery. Salvatore Vasta, who sells uniforms on an Internet site, hopes to be believed when he asserts that Anglo-Saxons have promulgated an image of the Italian soldier as "cowardly, inept . . . lazy [and] technologically and militarily backward." Yes, and it's notable that much Allied contempt for Italian troops (much of it, of course, baseless) has focused on uniforms alone. Dandies and losers the Italians were characterized as, and this reputation was earned less through combat behavior than through the traditional implications of textiles and tailoring and feathers. The blame for their lost war falls not just on the troops and their officers but on their fashion designers.

Admiral Zumwalt's Big Mistake

Meddling with classics usually backfires, bringing to the meddler shame rather than applause. The Bible, for example, is best in the original version: "Jesus wept" clearly beats "Jesus burst into a flood of tears," as one eighteenth-century translator improved John 11:35. Likewise, the traditional martini will be around longer than the chocolate one, and among film critics it is axiomatic that the original movie is superior to the remake. It's the same with uniforms, especially when they are so familiar as to seem an indispensable element of the setting.

This principle was sadly violated in the early 1970s. Admiral Elmo Zumwalt, the new young and energetic Chief of Naval Operations, noting that enlistments and re-enlistments in the Navy were declining drastically because of the unpopularity of the Vietnam War, ordered new and, in his view, more attractive uniforms for all his sailors. This was not the first time someone powerful wanted to change the sailors' uniform. In the Second World War, Admiral Ernest J. King, a vigorous hater of Britain, is said to have wanted to change the U.S. Navy enlisted men's uniform because it derived from, and still rather resembled, the British tars'. Admiral Zumwalt, for his part, wanted sailors to look more up-to-date and more like ordinary people.

★

THUS, HE ORDERED a total change in the bluejackets' uniform, beginning with a new white dress shirt with buttons and black necktie instead of the dark blue jumper with rectangular collar overlapping the shoulders. New also were ordinary black trousers with zipper fly instead of the wonderfully odd thirteen-buttoned "broad fall front," a feature that for countless years had made neat urination a most complex procedure, which it had been a matter of nautical pride to master. The thirteen buttons, by the way, do not, as folklore would have it, commemorate the thirteen original colonies. The number is purely accidental.

Now, the sailors when on liberty had to wear a dark blue jacket with brass buttons, like college boys in their blazers. There was also a navy blue windbreaker, of the sort known on golf courses. The whole new ensemble was topped off by a visor cap like the officers' or the chief petty officers'. This replaced the familiar round white one, which used to have expressive advantages: it could be worn well back on the head to register impudence or contempt but it could be properly squared on top of the head when an officer or CPO was around.

The new cap quickly earned the designation "the Donald Duck," for its resemblance to the cap worn by that personage. The hoped-for effect of these changes was to give every sailor the impression that he was already elevated to the rank of at least a chief, from whose uniform the ordinary tar's was now difficult to distinguish.

From the start, and to Elmo Zumwalt's surprise, the new uniform was thoroughly hated. One sailor commented: "The basic concept was that us enlisted types would have more self-esteem if our uniforms were similar to the chiefs' and officers'. I know one of the things I liked about the navy originally was never having to wear a tie (okay, we had the neckerchief but that isn't the same thing)." And, this thinker concluded, in a way surely astonishing to rationalists and reformers, "The classic bell bottoms, jumper, and white hat is, in my humble opinion [often abbreviated, in the Navy and elsewhere, IMHO], the sharpest dress uniform around." Some sailors wanted to retain the old style for less presentable reasons. They surfaced in the film *The Last Detail,* released, coincidentally, in 1973, the same year as Admiral Zumwalt's bright idea. Petty Officer Buddusky (played by Jack Nicholson) engages in conversation with a girl he's trying to impress, and finally, perceiving her total lack of interest, to offend:

> BUDDUSKY: I've seen things — I wouldn't even begin to tell you at a time like this, my fair darling.
>
> GIRL (with open contempt): I can see what it's done for you. . . . Must be the uniform.
>
> BUDDUSKY: They are cute, aren't they?
>
> GIRL: Oh, yeah.
>
> BUDDUSKY (looking down at his uniform trousers): You know what I like about it? One of my favorite things about this uniform is the way it makes your dick look.

(Robert Towne, author of the screenplay, deserves considerable credit for that line, IMHO.)

The new naval uniform lasted only five years. In 1978, Secretary of the Navy John Lehman, attentive to the sailors' objections to being made to look like something other than sailors, ordered a reversion to the old, traditional, much-loved style.

It's a pity that Admiral Zumwalt had to endure the embarrassment of being reversed, for he performed a number of good works. During his tenure as Chief of Naval Operations he bucked the Navy's habit of assigning African-American sailors only to kitchen work or to performing as waiters on officers' tables. He liberalized leave and liberty policy, allowed beer machines in shore quarters, and relaxed strict haircut and grooming regulations, permitting not just longer hair but sideburns — like his own. He opened his office for regular sailors' grievance sessions, and in many other ways eliminated what he called "demeaning and abrasive regulations." ("Navy regs" to the officers, "chicken-shit regs" to the sailors.) All this, of course, to the horror of countless reactionary and mostly retired admirals. But despite these brilliant reforms, Zumwalt never sufficiently understood the principle of unreason in normal life. He never understood the sailors' devotion to their beloved classic uniform. Oddly, they wanted to look not up-to-date but like Sailor Jack with his dog Bingo as depicted on the Crackerjack box.

It is painful to mention it, but there was another of Zumwalt's initiatives that backfired, and severely. It was he who ordered the use of Agent Orange in Vietnam, and it was his own son, a naval lieutenant whose assignment brought him into contact with that chemical, who died of cancer as a result — and whose son, in turn, undoubtedly from the same cause, proved hopelessly brain-damaged. To cap it all, Admiral Zumwalt himself died of a similar cancer. So considering the whole package of his ideas, reform of uniforms included, perhaps amusement is not an appropriate reaction. The irony might be better handled by Sophocles than by Jonathan Swift.

Once the Zumwalt years were past, with considerable relief the Navy resumed its time-honored ways, as a selection from current uniform regulations indicates. The regulations for the new female sailors have generated lots of comedy:

> Women's underpants/brassieres shall be white or skin color when wearing Whites.
>
> Pregnant women in the navy may wear outergarments (raincoat, overcoat, peacoat, reefer, and sweater) unbuttoned when they no longer fit buttoned.
>
> Earrings for women are an optional item. . . . When worn, the earring shall be a 4–6mm ball (gold for officers, silver for grades E-6 and below), plain with brushed, matte finish, shiny, screw-on type or post. Pearl earrings may be worn with Dinner Dress or Formal Uniforms.
>
> Women's berets are worn toward the front of the head, approx. ¾ of an inch from the forehead hairline, and tilted slightly to the right.
>
> Handbags are carried over the left shoulder or forearm, leaving the right arm and hand free for saluting. . . .

And the part in men's hair can no longer escape specific regulatory attention. "Men are authorized to have one . . . natural, narrow, fore-and-aft part in their hair. Hair cut or parted at an

unnatural angle is faddish and not authorized." Naval discipli-
narians are still loyal to the concept of the Gig Line. To avoid a
gig, or demerit, when wearing a cadet's or marine's uniform,
one's front should exhibit a regular unbroken line consisting of
the shirt buttons, the belt buckle, and the trouser fly.

The Navy doesn't lack its internal satirists, like the one who
conceived this: "Cutlasses are not authorized for wear by enlisted personnel." A joke, but it could almost be serious.

THERE'S CLEARLY SOMETHING about uniforms, and
about excessive veneration for them, that comes dangerously
close to silliness. One person dressed up, ready for serious publicly authorized business, may be impressive, but a large group
dressed all the same may be a little ludicrous because their appearance is so controlled and artificial. Inhuman, one might say.
So remote from the image of Huckleberry Finn.

Who can behold a symphony orchestra all in white tie and
tails without sensing something a bit funny in that anomalous
spectacle? Too like penguins, perhaps. But better to stick with
even the slightly ridiculous familiar than to dash into the un-
tried, as the conductor Leonard Bernstein learned in 1958,
when he decided that the white-tie outfit was inappropriate for
the New York Philharmonic — perhaps reasoning that it was
an incongruous uniform for an up-to-the-minute orchestra that
often played contemporary music. As a trial, he ordered the
evening clothes to be replaced, on Thursday nights, with blue
trousers and shirts and collarless blue jackets, like the "leisure
jackets" popular in America in the 1930s.

Of course, outrage arose, and after a fair number of Thurs-
days Bernstein was forced to return to the old style. He himself
finally designated the whole affair "Bernstein's Folly." Those
familiar with Renaissance writing and folklore may recall a
once-popular injunction: "Do not stir a standing turd."

Brass Buttons

The dress uniforms of military and naval personnel display many shiny buttons seldom seen on civilian dress. They are made of brass, of course, but in some high-class situations they may actually be gold-plated. They seem to appeal especially to boys and the boyish. One example from many: Henry Orenstein, about to enter secondary school in Poland in the 1930s and providentially unaware of his awful future, wrote, in his Holocaust memoir, "I was very excited about putting on my new blue uniform with gold buttons."

Booth Tarkington's *Penrod* — written, it is well to remember, in 1914, some time before anyone would predict the current era of political correctness and justice to minority citizens — took for granted the institutions of public racial segregation and general condescension. At one point Penrod and his friends consider the topic, What do you want to be when you grow up?

HERMAN: "I'm go' be a rai'road man! . . . Go' be a po'tuh! My uncle's a po-tuh right now. Solid gold buttons — oh, oh."
PENROD: "Generals got a lot more buttons than porters. . . ."
HERMAN: "Po-tuhs make the bes' livin'."

We can hardly be surprised, then, to find that perpetual adolescent boy, General George S. Patton, inordinately fond of brass buttons. In the Second World War his fellow Army commanders, wearing new waist-length "Eisenhower" jackets, were content to wear them virtually as issued, the necessary row of buttons on the front concealed by a vertical placket. Not Georgie. Following the seldom invoked tradition that a high general officer is allowed to design his own uniform, he had a tailor run him up a version of the Eisenhower jacket all his own, with four gilt buttons in a row down the front and two gilt buttons fastening the two breast-pocket flaps.

Regardless of this self-indulgent deviation from uniform convention, he insisted on maintaining a strict dress code in his Third Army. As far as I know, none of his equals called attention to this interesting inconsistency. They were also kind enough not to giggle at his habit of wearing in public a preposterous lacquered helmet liner, apparently betokening, in his view, his readiness to kill at all times and places.

His grandson, Robert H. Patton, who knew him about as well as anyone, noted that, despite his adult behavior in many ways, "throughout his life he displayed the exuberance and energy of a child, also the optimism and daring, the sentimentality, the fragile extreme emotionalism, the wide-eyed curiosity, the spiritual credulity . . . in short, the ingenuous spontaneity of unscarred and unchastened youth." "Patton is a problem child": that was the verdict of his superior officer, Dwight D. Eisenhower.

Gilt buttons have a long history of controversy because of their power to generate anger among those forbidden, by sumptuary law or by bourgeois taste, to wear them. In 1886 the Knights Templar of the United States were reprimanded by superior authority for having showy gilt buttons instead of the prescribed black on their uniform frock coats. Gilt buttons by that time were firmly established as an aristocratic emblem, ever since French King Francis I, in the sixteenth century, had appeared in a suit decorated with 15,000 gold buttons. And by the eighteenth century they were a well-known feature of gentlemen's coats and waistcoats. In the 1830s, each West Point cadet wore a waist-length black-tailed jacket with a high collar and three vertical rows of gilt buttons, one on the right, one on the left, and one in the center. All the rows began at the waist, but the ones on the sides of the chest made a V, ending at the shoulders, as if to delineate and emphasize the wearer's masculinity. (It's interesting, by the way, that gilt buttons always appear in some quantity, seldom alone, and usually in even numbers, balanced side by side. Captain E. J. Smith of the *Titanic* wore ten, in two vertical rows of five, as if in obedience to the principles of form and balance highly valued in the secure days before the Modernist period.)

The ability of gilt buttons to signal some sort of official status and authority became common during the nineteenth century, when steerage passengers immigrating to America were terrified by the approach of anyone on shipboard wearing gilt buttons. Keeping these buttons shined was more important in British services than in others. In the formal inquiry following the infamous Halifax riots in May 1945, when members of the Royal Navy expressed their joy at VE-day by running wild in the city, smashing windows, stealing liquor, and enjoying women in public, one authority declared: "It is true that those who have not been permitted to put their hands in their pockets for years are apt to do so as soon as they get out of uniform. Many would prefer not to be made to wear anything with brass buttons on it, or, if that fate is inescapable, develop an inclination not to Brasso them. But no known law of nature requires them to run amok."

The best-known American outlet for brass buttons is probably the Waterbury Button Company, located in Connecticut, the center of U.S. brass country. It has been manufacturing brass buttons since 1812, at first for American military services, then for many state police and fire departments, and finally for J. C. Penney. The green blazers worn by winners of the Masters golf tournaments bear Waterbury buttons, and Waterbury still supplies the Royal Navy, or what's left of it. All these buttons are made of solid brass, often plated with 24-carat gold. They will probably never lose their attraction to men who like to think their blazers give off, like their tennis sweaters, some yachtsmanly or upper-class resonance.

Generals' Dress

Perhaps George S. Patton did go too far, with his gilt buttons and lacquered helmet liner, but there may have been more to it than simple vanity. He had thought a lot about the relation of uniform to correct combat behavior and noted the strong element of individual pride attending each. The appearance of officers, he knew, was a powerful part of military leadership at the front. As he wrote, early in his career, "Officers must assert themselves by example and by voice. They must be pre-eminent in courage, deportment, and dress," with plenty of emphasis on the last item. A distinctive item of uniform — like his ivory-handled pistol — was for him an unignorable part of the apparatus of successful military action, indispensable in the art of making troops do what they don't want to do. And he was fully conscious of the theatrical element in all this.

He once told a subordinate, "As an officer you are always on parade," and insisted that "a little fancy dress" sustains the morale of those who witness it. During the battles in North Africa in 1943, he admitted to his diary that he was not always as brave as he seemed, and that he relied on his uniform to keep his courage up. As he put it, "I have to exude confidence I don't feel every minute." And after the invasion of Normandy, he wrote, "Have been wearing my shoulder holster. . . . so as to get myself into the spirit of the part." He died fourteen years before Erving Goffman's bright remark about the presentation of self, but if he'd ever come upon it, he would have whooped in joyful agreement. Attention to wardrobe is as necessary to winning as firepower and maneuver, and "generals," he declared, "must always be very neat."

From his earliest military days at the Virginia Military Institute Patton was hyperconscious of his looks, telling his parents not to send any more "canday" because he was trying to diet. His grandson observed that as a cadet Patton sometimes changed clothes more than ten times a day to keep his appearance absolutely uncriticizable. In the First World War he commanded the U.S. Tank Brigade, and on his return to that unit after spending some time in the hospital because of a nasty wound, his troops noted that his first circulated order was titled "Concerning dress, comportment and discipline of this command." He once sent General Pershing a memo, "Military Appearance and Bearing," reprehending the careless turnout of junior officers.

Just after the First World War he proposed a special uniform for the men of his tank brigade: green jodhpurs worn with a double-breasted, tight-fitting green jacket, on which gilt buttons ran diagonally from the waist to the right shoulder. The whole was to be topped with a football helmet decorated with a gold band. The historian Carlos D'Este writes that "when he posed in it for a group of photographers, he resembled a football player dressed as a bellboy." In the Second World War he told his diary, "Tomorrow I shall have my new battle jacket [probably the one with the gilt buttons]. If I'm to fight I like to be well dressed." And as the end of the war drew near, it was with an image of an officer's uniform that he delivered one final combative remark: "At the close of this war I will remove my insignia and wristwatch. I will continue to wear my short coat so that everyone can kiss my ass."

But in spite of all this theater, it's now possible, with the aid of a book like Roger Nye's *The Patton Mind,* to see a new complexity in Patton. During the long period of official boredom between the wars, he applied himself to a program, many years long, of serious reading in learned texts about war, leadership, and psychology. He wrote and filed thousands of index cards of scholarly notes on this reading. One book he annotated thoroughly and pleasurably was Gustave Le Bon's *The Crowd: A Study of the Popular Mind* (1896). There, as he noted, he learned "the advantage of a peculiar dress" in assisting the effectiveness of an orator's harangues.

He once said of his ivory-handled pistol that it was for social purposes only — he meant theatrical purposes. If he had ever needed a personal weapon, he had the .32-caliber Colt automatic he liked to wear under his shirt or carry in his right-hand trouser pocket.

ALTHOUGH, LIKE PATTON, he had a notable temper, Dwight Eisenhower also had something that Patton was weak in. Eisenhower came not from family money but from humble rural origins, and modesty, not bragging, was his forte. Sometimes he was capable of behavior for which "noble" is the only adequate term. Like his action while the invasion of Normandy was in progress and its outcome was still in doubt. Fearful that the whole enterprise could easily fail, he penciled on a sheet of notebook paper a statement to give the public if (when?) necessary: "Our landings in the Cherbourg-Havre area have failed to gain a satisfactory foothold and I have withdrawn the troops. My decision to attack at this time and place was based on the best information available." And he concluded this little document, which, thank God, never had to be used, with words that more than anything define his character and abundantly indicate his distance from Patton's boyish vainglory: "If any blame or fault attaches to this attempt, it is mine alone." (That sentence deserves to become a classic of American folk honor, carved on the façade of a dignified public building.)

Several times during the war Eisenhower had to deal with his friend Patton's misbehavior and soothe angry critics. Once, in Sicily, George slapped two soldiers he thought were malingering. Another time, he embarrassed the whole Allied cause by publicly asserting that England and America were going to rule the world after the war — and, even worse, omitted to mention Russia as part of the alliance. Finally, as postwar governor of Bavaria, he caused a scandal by making some pro-Nazi remarks — he really admired what he took to be Nazi efficiency, regardless of the movement's racial policies. This was finally too much, and Eisenhower had to get him out of the way; he assigned Patton to a harmless unit producing a history of the war.

Eisenhower was that rare creature, an honest man. He was a staff officer, not a combat leader. Because he was seldom physically in command of troops, he refused to enjoy the easy claim to courage implied by such devices as Patton's helmet liner and visible pistol. He wore instead headgear appropriate to the staff — what was then known as a service cap or garrison cap, with a leather visor. You could never imagine fighting in it, what with the gilt coat of arms of the United States shining on the front. Air Corps officers did wear it when fighting, but only when they were seated in their planes and had removed the grommet so that they could use their earphones. The service cap with the grommet removed — the Fifty Mission crush, this effect was called — conveyed so desirable an air of carelessness that many among the ground troops tried removing the grommet, an act forbidden by authority, often by brute insult and ridicule. Only the aviators were allowed this go-to-hell style, but, then, they sang gaily of going down in flame, something the ground troops never did.

Living in London as the commander in chief of Allied forces in Europe, Eisenhower had ample opportunity to see the British troops in their waist-length battle jackets, which for style, simplicity, and comfort clearly beat the American dress jacket. His naval aide, Harry C. Butcher, noted in May 1943 that

> Ike has been impressed by the virtual impossibility of American officers and soldiers appearing neat and snappy in their field uniforms. . . . He has suggested to General Marshall that the Quartermaster begin now to have designed another winter uniform for next winter's wear. He thought the material should be rough wool because it

wouldn't show the dirt and is more easily kept presentable. He liked the appearance of the British battle dress,
but thought Americans should design something distinctive for themselves.

At first Eisenhower thought of the jacket as a part of combat
dress, hence no gilded buttons. (For combat, the troops tended
to wear the dark green cotton field jacket with ample pockets
for storing K-ration boxes and extra ammunition.) Officially,
the new jacket was designated Wool Field Jacket M-1944, but it
quickly became known as the Eisenhower jacket, because the
general wore it, from the minute it was produced, when inspect-
ing soldiers. Immediately, everyone wanted one. The British
wool battle jacket was made of rough, rather ugly, apparently
unfinished material. When the Americans produced something
like it, they unconsciously raised its status by manufacturing it
from the same smooth, classy wool used in the former dress
jacket, worn with shirt and tie. The Eisenhower jacket turned
out to look surprisingly stylish, and it soon became a favored
part of the dress uniform for officers and men alike.

Eisenhower had a reputation among the troops as an eminently decent man, friendly and sympathetic, and that reputation certainly helped establish the popularity of the garment
named for him. For one thing, he had the guts to violate the sacred Army injunction against being seen with your hands in
your pockets. It is hard to imagine any article of uniform named
after the hated and feared Patton. His shiny helmet liner never
caught on, even among the most vain and insensitive of officers,
although some photos survive showing Omar Bradley looking
very silly in one.

Eisenhower made a further contribution to army uniform.
Butcher testified, "General Ike ordered that all officers commanding combat troops . . . shall be allowed to wear a distinctive narrow green [felt] band around the shoulder loops of his
uniform. . . . He wants this distinctive marking to set apart combat officers and men from those officers and enlisted personnel
who are on staff duty." Sergeants leading their men into mortal

battle got to wear, as an indicator, a narrow green stripe below the chevrons on their sleeves. Once it was discovered how dangerous infantry combat was, these little tokens were highly valued by those allowed to wear them, especially later, when the men went on leave in Paris or Nancy and were mistaken (insultingly) for personnel in such safe units as quartermaster, finance, and transportation. These green tokens were never sufficiently publicized, however, and few civilians knew what they meant or knew the kind of fear and agony that had made them necessary.

They were still being worn, or supposed to be worn, in Vietnam, and the Army felt it necessary to declare that "the combat leader's identification" was to be worn "only by personnel having leadership positions in units with direct combat missions." Staff officers and men were strictly forbidden to wear them, and in May 1970, apparently fed up with reports of these significant green loops being worn by command sergeants major, who were considered staff members rather than combat leaders, the high command unequivocally ordered such men to take off the green loops and quit posing. The only high World War II officer I've seen photographed wearing these things was Omar Bradley, and doubtless in his own mind he deserved them. But modest and honest Eisenhower did not wear them, just as he never appeared in a helmet.

IT IS SAID to have been the example of Eisenhower that persuaded Douglas MacArthur finally to simplify his uniform in the direction of understatement. MacArthur had arrived in Australia in 1942 sporting all his ribbons and exhibiting even his Expert Rifleman's Badge. But when a newspaper printed a picture of Ike wearing no decorations at all, MacArthur apparently decided that Ike's was to be the new style. Henceforth for most occasions MacArthur reformed, appearing in khaki trousers and an open-collared, tieless shirt, without decorations, thus setting a "Pacific War" style, which others were delighted to adopt because of the heat and humidity, and also because they hankered after a uniform that was less formal than any previously available. The pictures of the Japanese surrender on the deck of the U.S.S. *Missouri* are some of the most significant of the whole war: the triumphant Allied officers in their informal, unpretentious khakis, pressing forward for a sight of the humiliated, overdressed Japanese officers and diplomats wearing standard hot uniforms and striped trousers, black tailcoats, and silk top hats.

MacArthur's simple khaki shirt and trousers are especially interesting, because formerly he had been one of the leading peacocks in the United States Army. Returning from the First World War, he had himself photographed in a showy collegiate raccoon coat with a long wool scarf that had been knitted by his doting mother. On top, his unchanging trademark, his grommetless, gold-bullion embroidered service cap. Helping to drive the bonus marchers out of Washington in 1932, he came on in full dress uniform, with Sam Browne belt, riding breeches and boots, and ribbons rising to the shoulder of his jacket. When he was installed as Field Marshal of the Philippine Forces, he appeared in a uniform of his own vain design: black trousers, white jacket covered with medals, ribbons, badges, and gold cords. Hastily leaving Bataan in 1942, he was wearing loud-checked civilian socks and brown wing-tipped low shoes with decorative little holes. Finally, at the end of his years, he directed that he be buried in his faded khakis without decorations or badges, wearing on his unbuttoned collar only the little circlets of five stars. He wanted to go out, he explained, in the khakis that "have been part of my soul," the emblem of his proudest achievements, winning the Pacific War and, as a sort of lay emperor, democratizing Japan. He said of his khaki uniform, "Whatever I've done that really matters I've done wearing it."

A QUESTION. Is flagrant eccentricity a cause of a person's rising to high command in the military, or is the position itself, obliging the holder constantly to consider the best ways of killing people, so deeply dyed with irrationality as to cause personal eccentricity? Few could deny that Patton was an eminent weirdo, and few could overlook MacArthur's oddities — the intense egotism, the automatic assumption of his own rectitude, the pompous oratorical stance on all occasions. But with Sir Bernard Law Montgomery, general and ultimately field marshal, hero of El Alamein, designated viscount by his sovereign, one enters the precincts of human oddity raised to all but the highest power. Consider: all who had to deal with him noticed and hated his almost pathological egotism, his lack of sensitivity in his neglect of his son and his bizarre hatred of his mother, his psychological insecurity resulting in his terror of being criticized in any way, his instinct for bullying, and his boastful insubordination, which once drew this rebuke from the nice-natured Eisenhower: "Steady, Monty. You can't speak to me like that. I'm your boss." Probably what really annoyed Montgomery was the impudence of Ike, this one-time pre–1776 colonial (almost "native") of the United Kingdom, giving orders to Monty's own sacred country, now enfeebled and bankrupt.

But he was complicated and contradictory. He tended to reserve his contempt for the Americans and the French, yet was kindness itself to his own troops, and he exercised extraordinary military wisdom. He had been brought to North Africa to relieve General Auchinleck, commander of the Eighth Army, who had shown little ability to conquer Rommel's forces. When he arrived, he concluded that he must quickly raise the morale of the troops. Although a bigoted nonsmoker, he passed out cigarettes and was not avid in discouraging drinking and whoring, so long as the men won their battles. He moved often among them, garbed at first in an Australian bush hat, fastened up on one side (he had grown up in Tasmania), and later in a black beret, worn with a heterodox two badges (only one was authorized), one the emblem of the tankers, the other his own insignia as a general. He explained what he was going to do when he attacked, and the men listened, satisfied that a leader had at last taken them into his confidence. He somehow made his perverse egotism theirs, performing this bit of theater with amazing skill. One brigadier later recalled his first sight of Montgomery in the desert: "He was very small, very skinny, this little man. He was more comic than anything else. A sort of foxy face. He had a very unfortunate, rather spinsterly voice, rather high-pitched." But "this startling little performer" acted in such a way as to make confidence credible and victory in the coming battle virtually assured.

At the same time, those in close official contact with him agreed that "he wasn't a nice man," but agreed also that nice men don't win battles. At first he wore correct uniform, with a tall row of ribbons on his battle-dress jacket. But gradually he replaced that with a markedly less official *tenue*. When the former actor Lieutenant M. E. Clifton James, of the Pay Corps — who had the task of impersonating Montgomery in a scheme designed to mislead the enemy about his whereabouts — saw the general for the first time, he was prepared to study and finally mimic his voice, gestures, and posture, but he found himself seriously unprepared for the man's deviations from prescribed uniform. Once, his railway train was standing near a row of official cars, and Monty and staff appeared. James recalled his shock:

> Ever since I had held a commission I had been under the shadow of strict discipline, and I had imagined that on H.Q. staff the discipline would be even stricter. Yet here were officers wearing battle-dress blouses, suede shoes, and corduroy slacks of many colors. When Monty appeared I understood why his staff wore colored corduroys. Their chief was similarly dressed with a gray roll-top [i.e., turtleneck] sweater and of course the black beret.

Later, Lieutenant James was summoned into Monty's presence, where he experienced something thoroughly startling. "As we stood facing each other it was rather like facing myself in a mirror."

In addition to cords, Montgomery was partial to sleeveless sweaters and tennis shoes, the whole outfit tending to suggest the sensibleness and normality of the war, its proximity to familiar civilian usages. Sometimes in the desert the only autho-

rized item Monty wore was the black beret, made unauthorized
by the two badges. As the novelist and wartime major Anthony
Powell observed of Monty, "His personality was not adapted to
military chic." It was in this low-down uniform of baggy cords
and sweater that Montgomery chose to receive the four German officers who had come to present their surrender. Monty's
personal assistant recalled the scene. "Though defeated, they
looked overpoweringly sinister in their jackboots and long
black leather overcoats. Monty, deliberately, was dressed at his
most casual, wearing a pair of corduroy trousers that had been
washed so many times that they were bleached white and had
no crease."

The wearer of this ensemble took the opportunity to deliver
a few choice insults: "Who are you? I have never heard of you."
When one of the Germans was introduced as a Major, Monty
affected to fly into a paroxysm of military snobbery. "Major!
How dare you bring a Major into my headquarters?" But the
next day, when the surrender document was to be signed,
Monty ended this pleasing satire and appeared "sprucely clad"
in his tailor-made battle dress blouse with ribbons. His normal dress was a bit like MacArthur's tieless khakis in the Pacific: comfy, businesslike, and — like the untraditional A-bomb
— effective. Both the MacArthur khakis and the Montgomery
cords and sweater suggest appropriate combat wear for modern times: the best uniform for the highly athletic work of killing would be jeans and sweatshirts (T-shirts in hot weather).
There's an American precedent for that sort of thing. For those
fighting in the American Revolution, the European uniforms
were so heavy and awkward that many were felled by heat
stroke. "Among the German troops," writes the historian Na-
than Joseph, "was a dismounted cavalry regiment compelled to
tramp through New York and New England forests during the
very hot summer of 1777 while wearing heavy leather breeches,
high boots, spurs, and trailing long sabers." No wonder the
"Americans" won that war: when it grew hot, they fought in
their shirts.

Blue Jeans

Freedom from convention. That was originally the message to be conveyed by the institution of blue jeans, which, like jazz, Hollywood, and Coca-Cola, is one of America's most impressive inventions. But when everyone has at least one pair, what do you have? A uniform, and just as much a uniform as the dark suit. True, some escape from all-but regulatory uniformity may be had by adhering to variations on the standard Levi's, such as painters' white coveralls and carpenters' specials, with hammer loops. Bib overalls also offer momentary escape from the blue denim convention, especially when worn in places where they are most likely to occasion surprise — stockbrokers' premises, for example, pulpits, or funerals. But still, the authority of real blue jeans (waist overalls, as they were called at first) is illustrated by the wild success of the Levi Strauss product and its countless imitators.

The Levi's success story has been retailed almost to death, but once more may be pardoned. "Levi Strauss" was originally not a brand name but an actual boy born in Bavaria. He arrived in America with his parents in 1847. His older brother was already here, engaged in the New York dry-goods trade. The Gold Rush of 1849 attracted them to the West Coast, and they settled in San Francisco, where they founded a branch of the eastern business.

Gold miners, successful or not, required heavy-duty trousers, and the younger Strauss boy began manufacturing them from brown canvas, a thick version of which was made in New Hampshire. When the stock ran out, he moved on to blue denim. At first, the seams were merely sewn and didn't hold very long. But soon an inventor sold the Strausses the idea of using copper rivets to reinforce the seams, and their product took off. (Probably only a psychiatrist could figure out the relation between those rivets and the popular, if unpublicized, idea of masculinity.) Cone Mills, in North Carolina, has won the modern contract for supplying the denim. Once, in Raleigh, when I noticed the constant noise of large aircraft overhead, I was told that cargo planes were conveying bolts of blue denim in immense quantities to manufacturers no longer in San Francisco but in cheap-labor Central America.

When the Gold Rush had run its course, cowboys became popular, and the jeans passed to them and their impersonators on their way to America's youth, who wanted to annoy their stuffy parents. Until around 1963, part of the routine for Levi's wearers was shrinking the trousers to fit, and the best way to do that was to put them on wet and let them dry on your body. This gave the wearer the impression that he or she was actually creating the garment, or at least emphasizing one's precious individuality, and that conviction did nothing to oppose the illusion of uniqueness precious to all American young people. Writing in the 1970s, Alison Lurie, in her excellent study *The Language of Clothes,* could say, "Ninety percent of middle-class and college students of both sexes are now identical below the waist, though above they may wear anything from a lumberjack shirt to a lace blouse."

The Levi Strauss company did so well out of this primitivist, class-war impulse that its goods ultimately ravished the youth of Europe and Asia, and it became the largest clothing maker in the world. Before long it was supplying other nonformal but uniform-like garments — bell bottoms and blue denim jackets and skirts — and it finally branched out into making khaki trousers, which rapidly became as popular among college students as blue jeans once had been. "Stone-washing" and bleaching kept Levi's at the front of the leisure-wear trade, and the company did very well, until baggy pants began to replace jeans. Next to cigarettes and booze, Levi's were the one product most frequently highjacked, and the one most frequently counterfeited.

One question will torment anyone considering the meaning of blue jeans. What, in addition to their anti-parent and anti-respectability function, made them catch on so intensely and become an unignorable feature of American actuality? In short, why? Yes, they were cheap, but what else?

As usual, there is a sexual, or at least a pelvic, answer. Because of the tight-fitting crotch and rear, jeans became an indispensable part of a young man's dating and seduction equipment. (A possibly instructive contrast with the tight jeans of a young man on the make would be the anti-sexual garb of monks and friars, with notably loose robe and rope belt.) Allied with the new freedom from pregnancy anxiety provided by the pill, jeans ushered in an entirely new world of pleasure for the young. And if they were carefully worn by women, the tight seam in front could delineate, even through the thick fabric, the labia majora and similar attractions. But jeans still were considered largely a male garment, and after James Dean and Marlon Brando wore them in their extravagantly popular films about types of social rebellion, their success was sexually assured. Schools began banning jeans, finding them (correctly) occasions of misrule and troublemaking. As early as the 1950s or thereabouts, the wearing of jeans, especially in inappropriate contexts, became one of the pop styles of anti-fashion.

But, ironically, starting out as an impudent antidote to uniform, they became the most important — and finally square — uniform of all. At first you wore them with the cuffs turned up a few inches, achieving a "cowboy" look. (Real cowboys did this the better to display their costly cowboy boots.) But in 1950 normal people ceased turning up the cuffs — nobody knows why. Nor what motivated boys to go in for cutting off a good bit of the legs. That uniform was in due course replaced by baggy jeans, affected by skateboard addicts and similar pseudo-degenerates. Before long, pedantry required that every detail be correct — that is, uniform. And soon there came along Calvin Klein's "dirty jeans," with faux mud stains and embarrassing food bits already printed on the denim. And as people in the fashion trade know all too well, there are now Torn and Mended Jeans, jeans held together with safety pins (priced at $2,222), jeans with built-in creases, jeans inscribed with graffiti, and various costly brands of "designer jeans" (in the trade, "embellished jeans"), clean and neat and decorated with embroidery, rhinestones, beads, nail heads, and sequins. Of this decadent practice one Levi Strauss spokesman declared that the garments "had lost their essential jeansiness."

But the genuine article will doubtless persist as long as adolescents find cause to annoy their parents and as long as employees on casual-dress days and pop stars choose to signal their contempt for uniforms by wearing the most familiar uniform of all. As usual, a device for flaunting an anti-fashion stance, with appropriate political and intellectual implications, ends as an obligatory style. We can reason that there is finally no escape.

PROBABLY FEARING TO be classified as mere "fashion" journalists (a despicable breed, to be sure), serious writers and thinkers have tended to avoid close study of the jeans phenomenon. One who took the risk is Umberto Eco. In his essay "Lumbar Thought," he found the subject of jeans "rich in philosophical reflections," which he proposed to explore, holding that "no everyday experience is too base for the thinking man."

Assuming that jeans worn by men must be very tight-fitting, he discovered that in his new jeans, his body was divided into two "independent zones," one, the shirt and jacket part above, relatively free-moving, and the other, below the belt line, pleasantly constricted by the jeans, as if by a lower-body corset. He experienced a new feeling arising from the sense that he had imposed a sort of armor on his lower body, especially his sexual zone. Self-consciousness about his jeans moved him toward a new relation with the external world. "I had achieved hetero-consciousness, that is to say, an epidemic self-awareness." This idea led him to some certainly doubtful reasoning, or mock-reasoning, about the effect of tight-fitting garments on intellectual ambition and achievement. Tight-lacing, he speculated, may have interfered with the originality and rapidity of thought among women before the modern era. Perhaps. But tight-lacing among corset-wearing dandies certainly had no such effect. In opposition to Eco's notion, I'd say that the only effect of wearing tight jeans on the middle-aged and elderly is a false conviction of recovered youth. But that illusion can be, as many will confirm, dangerous.

The Rise and Fall of the Brown Jobs

It's not easy to grasp the problem of the American military uniform without awareness of a very different tradition elsewhere. The novelist Simon Raven likes to depict moments of acute uniformitis among the British. Here's a bit from his recall, in *Fielding Gray,* of a memorial service in his school chapel two days after V-E day. The school had invited its alumni,

> and the visitors' pews were crowded with uniforms. While all of us were wearing scruffy gray flannels and patched tweed jackets, the champions of England were hung about with every color and device. . . . There were the black and gold hats of the guardsmen, the dark-green side-caps of the rifles, kilts swaying from the hips of the highlanders, and ball buttons sprayed all over the horse artillerymen; there were macabre facings and curiously knotted lanyards; there were even the occasional boots and spurs, though these were frowned on in 1945 because of Fascist associations. . . . I myself had a place in the Sixth Form block which commanded a good view of the visitors, and I could see [by the middle of the memorial service] that the magnificent officers were openly preening themselves. . . . Indeed, when the roll of the dead was called (a proceeding which took some time), there were unmistakable signs of boredom and pique; there was much fingering of canes and riding whips, much fidgeting with Sam Browne belts.

Ultimately Raven found himself enrolled in an eccentric but by no means rare regiment that, before the age of the tank, had been a cavalry unit, and this presumed social distinction was never forgotten, especially, as mentioned in *Feathers of Death,* in the details of the uniform. "All officers . . . habitually wore service dress with riding boots, breeches and spurs, while other ranks wore tight trousers and spurs. . . . Our full dress . . . was of scarlet . . . but the headdress to go with it was a busby worn with a plume of feathers of royal purple."

No one who has served as an officer in any unit of the British army seems ever to lose his interest in the social language of uniform, even civilian ones. Anthony Powell, writing in his diary about the televised wedding ceremony of Prince Andrew and Miss Sarah Ferguson, pronounced it an "unusually good show . . . The bride's father . . . had braid piping on his tailcoat. As he is not old enough for this to have been a normal fashion for tailcoats . . . one presumes him still wearing the coat he had at Eton when in Pop, braid being a Pop privilege. It would be interesting to check on this." Reviewing two books on military uniforms of the First World War, Powell revealed his fascination with uniform details:

> The text and illustrations of these two books are good, but, in the case of the British, the latter sometimes misleadingly captioned, that is to say exceptional cases are not so noted. For example, a Brigadier General is shown wearing another rank's cap without a red band. This may well have been done (as explained in the note) but should be established as unusual. In the same manner, the caption says, "Foot Guards officer," which is in fact a Foot Guards officer on the staff, as he wears red tabs, though with the Guard's varying button-spacing on the tunic.

And every vagary, like the significantly different placing of tunic buttons from regiment to regiment, has its history, proudly recalled. Of course Powell was alert to one corollary of all this consciousness of regulated dress: eccentric behavior in league with dress conventions. Witness his depiction of retired Major George Fosdick, in his novel *From a View to a Death*. When many elderly gentlemen might take their afternoon nap, the major pursues a different course:

> This was his hour. The time to please himself. A period of mental relaxation. He went upstairs to his dressing-room and when he arrived there he locked the door. Then he turned to the bottom drawer of his wardrobe, where he kept all his oldest shooting-suits. He knelt down in front of this and pulled it open. Below the piles of tweed was a piece of brown paper and from under the brown paper he took two parcels tied up with string. Major Fosdick undid the loose knots of the first parcel and took from it a large picture-hat that had no doubt been seen at Ascot some twenty years before. The second parcel contained a black sequin evening dress of about the same date. Removing his coat and waistcoat, Major Fosdick slipped the evening dress over his head and, shaking it so that it fell down into position, he went to the looking-glass and put on the hat. When he arranged it at an angle that was to his satisfaction, he lit his pipe and, taking a copy of *Through the Western Highlands with Rod and Gun* from the dressing table, he sat down. In this costume he read until it was time to change for dinner. For a good many years now he had found it restful to do this for an hour or two every day when he had the opportunity. He himself would have found it difficult to account for such an eccentricity to anyone he might have happened to encounter during one of these periods, and it was for this reason that he was accustomed to gratify his whim only at times when there was a reasonable expectation that his privacy would be respected by his family. Publicly he himself would refer to these temporary retirements from the arenas of everyday life as his Forty Winks.

And here is Raven again, in *Sabre Squadron*, imagining a fictional regiment, Earl Hamilton's Light Dragoons, which he makes entirely believable. An officer of the dragoons explains:

We wear decorative trousers of a deep pink because Lord Hamilton was in his rose garden when he received his commission; and we call them "cherry" out of deference to William IV, who had the story wrong and thought it was a cherry orchard. In the winter we wear riding cloaks lined with silk of the same color and trimmed with collars of white fur, to buy one of which absorbs the whole of an officer's uniform allowance for about ten years.

From the glories of such full-dress uniforms as these, what a humiliating descent to actual daily wear, especially during the two World Wars, with their conscription of hundreds of thousands of non-high-class officers and unenthusiastic enlisted men. A character in Kurt Vonnegut's *Slaughterhouse-Five* is identified as a Nazi war criminal, but his hostile view of the American enlisted man's uniform is not far off the mark: "The American army," he declares, "sends its enlisted men out to fight and die in a modified business suit quite evidently made for another man, a sterilized but unpressed gift from a nose-holding charity which passes out clothing to drunks in the slums." The color of the general woolen uniform, worn by all ranks, was something like earth, adopted for the purposes of camouflage, not show or morale. In the States it was called olive drab. It was a shade that might have reminded an imaginative observer of the color of vomit or even excrement. British airmen and sailors started numerous pub fights by calling soldiers "Brown Jobs," a term of insult with fairly clear excremental implications. Even women, more polite, referred to the Drab Tommies.

A transsexual prostitute in Lincoln Kirstein's poem "Gloria" says to a sailor that you

> . . . simply cannot beat
> your Navy blue-and-gold or that old Navy neat-

> Nesses. You All look ssoo Damn *clean*. Why does the Army *never*
> in spite of all them soapy showers look Ever
> *clean?* . . .

In addition, the color could prompt misapprehensions about the wearer's identity. One American soldier, traveling by train in the 1930s, was addressed by a man who said, "I think it's wonderful the way some of you guys give freely of your time to the Boy Scouts." Even if in the Second World War American officers had the relief of wearing their stylish dress pinks and greens (trousers of a gray-pink shade, jackets of dark green and brown), for the men there was no escape from the old uniform, attended by all the time-honored insults.

It was not the intellectual and aesthetic erosion of the idea of military grandeur that led to the disuse of flashy uniforms. It was the utilitarian discovery that troops better survived the new techniques of military murder if they could hardly be seen. Thus, they wore earth or grass or fog-colored clothing. It is the theory and practice of camouflage, and not any shame about the vulgarity of showing off, that replaced gaudiness with the loathsome olive-drab uniform. Back in the eighteenth century soldiers needed to be seen in all their threatening glory to demoralize their enemy a short distance away. Now they needed to be unseen.

But the discovery of the camouflage principle opened a new problem, this time one of expenditure. Formerly, the soldier was given a fancy uniform for all purposes, but now he would have preferred at least two: one to fight in and one for walking out and taking girls on dates, clearly difficult when he risked being stigmatized as a Brown Job. But the hideous, socially inappropriate uniform had to serve all purposes. No wonder young men turned away and headed for the Marine Corps instead.

It was largely color shame that prompted the U.S. Army in 1946 to set about devising a wholly new uniform that might reinvigorate recruiting. In addition, a new uniform was necessary because anybody could buy an "Ike" jacket in a military surplus store and wear it while garbage-truck laboring or ditch-digging. And in those days lots of people wanted to demean the Army and satirize its presumably high purposes. The officers were already provided for with their pinks and dark greens, so most agitation for a new uniform came from the ranks. It wasn't just the revulsion from dirt-colored wool, but also a rejection of the warm-weather outfit, the cotton khaki trousers and shirt hard to distinguish from the outfits worn by repair men or delivery men. Popular was this little jest. General Patton arrives at a training camp to inspect a troop recreation room. It is summer. One khaki-clad man turns his back on him. Patton: "Don't you come to attention when an officer enters the room?" Delivery man: "Fuck you, buddy. I came in from town to refill the Coke machine."

As even the Army itself realized, its soldiers were "the most poorly dressed enlisted men in the military services, particularly on coat-and-tie occasions or on travel." And actually, there's plenty of evidence from well before the 1940s that the brighter soldiers were no enthusiasts for the uniform. A survey asking "Which do you prefer to wear on furlough, uniform or civilian clothes?" revealed, embarrassingly, that the worst educated men favored the uniform.

Perhaps it doesn't need to be stated that no uniform, no matter how humble, materializes out of the blue. Every one today is the product of prolonged thought, not just about the mission of the branch of service being outfitted but about the meanings of masculinity and femininity associated with that branch's functions and authority. Every uniform, as Cynthia Enloe, a professor of government, makes clear, has a politics as well as a history. The politics of any new uniform after the Second World War clearly had to be egalitarian. The troops wanted to look as much as possible like officers, especially officers clad in their chic pinks and greens. This motif was similar to the one dominating Admiral Zumwalt's experiment. Another stimulus for change was the appearance in 1949 of the Air Force's new light blue uniform, practically alike for officers and men. A further "political" motive was the desire, not often publicly voiced, to break away from apparent reliance on models furnished by Europe, especially the British, whose battle-dress jacket had inspired the Eisenhower imitation. It was as if Americans after the Second World War felt confident of their ability to go it alone.

It's almost as if someone in military authority had happened upon Emerson's essay "Self-Reliance" (1841) and perceived that it could apply to nations as well as persons.

Planners of the new uniform conceived of themselves at work on something revolutionary: the first permanent uniform for the army. All the preceding ones had been strictly ad hoc, expedients for one war only. Since historically the U.S. military has operated not as a large standing army but as a limited cadre expandable in time of need (that is, for World Wars), for each war it contrived a temporary uniform, training manufacturers in its rapid production.

The Army tried to make itself aware that it was doing something novel in devising a permanent uniform. It announced that it was "building a uniform tradition with the . . . Green Army Uniform." Unlike the Navy, whose uniforms reflect British naval usages of two centuries ago, the Army was deliberately going to produce a uniform that would not need changing. But even if it succeeded, problems would remain, most of them associated with the gradual Europeanization of the military uniform. The beret is replacing a variety of other headgear, and such uniquely American items like the Smoky Bear hat are on the way out, retained only by Marine Corps drill instructors. But lest we go overboard in assigning anything like taste to the military, there's the new generals' hyper-full-dress outfit, dark blue, with admirals' two-inch gold stripes on the cuffs, space for six rows of ribbons on the chest, and Civil War–style gold-and-blue epaulets turned sideways over the shoulders and displaying the wearer's rank within a gold rectangle. But the full-dress generals' cap is the prizewinner in the vulgarity sweepstakes: showy gold bullion "scrambled eggs" on both visor and crown. Costumed thus, General John Shalikashvili looked less like an army officer of high rank than a doorman at a pretentious restaurant or the man at the expensive hotel's curbside who solicits tips for helping you out of your vehicle. The principle of the generals' uniform is excess, as if the audience is too stupid to be impressed by anything less than the proudest display.

But back to the more ordinary, new green uniform. It took

years to produce, with contributions technical and aesthetic from thousands of people, including the man who developed, after elaborate trials, the color of green (Shade 44) finally adopted. He and many others were supervised by a major general heading the U.S. Army Supply and Maintenance Command in Washington. Contributors of ideas and help were the National Academy of Science; the Mellon Institute of Industrial Research; Hart, Schaffner, and Marx, and many other men's clothing makers; and the Rogers Peet company for tips about laundering and cleaning. Hattie Carnegie was appointed to design the new woman's uniform, assisted by Lord & Taylor, together with the editors of *Vogue* and *Harper's Bazaar*. With a committee this large, no wonder the process took so long. It wasn't until 1954 that the new uniform was ready to be approved by the troops, and not until 1961 that it became mandatory. Gone was the Army's historical dependence on the color brown, which had generated so many lewd jokes. The shoes to be worn with the green uniform were black, like the neckties.

The egalitarian impulse was not successful everywhere, for the chin strap on the officers' visor cap was now "gold," the men's only black, and the officers were permitted a black stripe on their trousers. Finally, the traditional army had to yield a bit more: field-grade officers (majors and colonels) got to display gold bullion patterns on their visors, just like generals, while generals could go a step farther, with an elaborate gold pattern around the base of the cap itself.

But there was more to the new uniform than the shirts and trousers, jackets and caps. Now there were cosy sweaters in pullover style, with shoulder bars (sliding black loops) on the shoulder straps depicting rank for officers and men alike. And there was also a lightweight version of the uniform for summer wear, as well as a new raincoat and overcoat. We should not, however, imagine that the new uniform somehow overcame the traditional Army skepticism and disgust. With nothing to bitch about, it would seem that soldiers lost their authenticity. An enlisted man, Wes Harris, said recently, "The current forest-green

Class A uniform is just awful with its accompanying mint-green shirt."

While this new army uniform was being born, the Air Force, no longer a mere branch of the army but, like the RAF, an independent arm, had to declare its independence by designing its new uniform. Secretary of the Air Force Stuart Symington was heard to say, "For God's sake, let's not have ODs, because it means Olive Drab. And it means *drab*. That's the thing we ought to stay away from." The United States fliers had long despised the Eisenhower jacket, holding that it made them resemble bus drivers. The necessity of distinguishing clearly members of the Air Force from the Brown Jobs (now cleansed into Green Jobs) required some originality, but the Air Force found it couldn't stray very far from the British model — light blue with silver-colored buttons. After considerable testing and talking, the official color was settled upon, officially designated Uxbridge 1693, also known as Shade 84 Blue.

In 1950 the new Air Force uniform was ready. There was little difference between the outfits of officers and men except the insignia. But the Air Force found it did have to make one significant change. The old tradition of manly shoulder patches would have to go. Some of the old ones had been openly warlike, if not sadistic, depicting skulls, demons, devils, and pirates. But the new shoulder patches were politically corrected, and one squadron, which had prided itself on its emblem of a pirate wearing the conventional eye patch, had to get rid of the eye patch, lest someone visually challenged be offended. Not merely a hitherto unheard-of egalitarianism, this new sentimentality was beginning to dominate the world of military uniforms, and soon the idea that the function of soldiers was to kill human beings, sometimes including women and children, became profoundly embarrassing, if not unthinkable.

But soldiers had to perform exercises in the field when training for their serious murderous work, and here a new combat uniform, far different from the walking-out get-up and dress outfit, was developed. It was named Battle Dress or Combat Fatigues. Everyone is familiar with this uniform, worn by many of the soldiers in Vietnam and locally by the National Guard. Its essence is fabric bearing a variety of camouflage patterns in four colors. The hope was that the infantrymen would look like leaves or some natural flora and thus deceive the enemy. Commanders have four patterns from which to choose, officially designated "Woodland," "Desert," "Arctic," and "Urban," this last imitating building surfaces like stucco, concrete, and brick. The whole idea may have reached America by way of the attire of many German troops in the Second World War, memorably encountered in Normandy, in what the poet Louis Simpson called their "leopard suits." Some U.S. soldiers tried similar dress in that war, but it was found that the American and German versions were so much alike that American troops shot one another. Regardless, the camouflage battle dress has persisted, and now all over the world ground troops look alike, a considerable difficulty, one might think, in the conduct of ground warfare. The *New York Times* is fond of depicting female models wearing battle-dress camouflage prints, and one of their photo captions, HOW NOT TO BLEND IN, unwittingly suggests the problems that will arise when all armies are clad the same — in camouflage patterns indistinguishable from each other. (In passing, it may be noted that some "couture" gowns made from camouflage fabrics are priced at $30,000.) And in New York, men are assumed to be as silly as women. That's the only conclusion to be drawn from an ad in the *New York Times* promoting a Burberry ensemble of underwear for males. It features a boldly camouflaged sleeveless T-shirt, and, in stretch cotton, "square-cut trunks." Or, as *trunks* seems to suggest, is it really swimwear?

It's not exactly clear why, stateside, U.S. troops are forbidden to wear battle dress in off-post places serving alcohol, but we are left to infer moments of civilian outrage in such places, leading to fights. The baggy behind of the battle dress coverall is hardly an effect conducive to dignity and impressiveness. So ubiquitous has become the impulse to camouflage everything that there are condoms printed in camouflage patterns, presumably to merge with the ground cover after a rape and thus conceal the presence of U.S. troops in the area.

American soldiers in the twentieth century have always had a fatigue uniform of gray-green cotton designed normally for wear during some kind of physical work, and these fatigue clothes were often worn in battle. But by the time of the Vietnam War, the movement to dress down everywhere, in offices as well as on battlefields, was well under way. In Vietnam, for example, informality and the need to address human actualities produced the official combat scarf, issued for wiping off sweat.

Now, the woolen light brown uniform that almost all armies affected at the beginning of the twentieth century has overtaken and sent into museums dress white jackets, fringed epaulets, and plumes on headdresses. There's been too much exposé of what really happens when physical violence has its way at sea, on the ground, and in the air, and fancy uniforms can no longer provide insulation against actuality. Which is to say that military romanticism has largely gone out, and even the bagpiper leading a group of soldiers is likely to be playing not "Scotland the Brave" but "Amazing Grace."

THE POWER OF the brown to expunge all trace of charm or even attractiveness can be seen in some American postage stamps issued in 2000. They were designed to commemorate and honor a number of famous soldiers of the Army ground forces — Omar Bradley, Audie Murphy, Alvin York, and the like. Even with the presence in a corner of a red or green divisional or Army patch for each soldier, the effect, because of the uniform brown, is uniformly obnoxious. It can give the innocent some idea of how depressing it must have been to wear the uniform of the Brown Jobs.

And something more comic than depressing. In the American Army, despite the attempt to establish a permanent outfit, nothing related to uniform stays unchanged for very long. The year 2001 saw the memorable Battle of the Berets, occasioned by the Army's attempt to put the entire congregation of arms and services into black berets. This headwear would replace the former "overseas cap," the flat one, which opens out to be worn tilted over the right eyebrow. Alluding to this classic bit of uniform, familiar since World War I, the *New York Times* asserted that soldiers called it the dunce cap. Quite wrong. It in no way resembled the tall, pointed dunce cap. It resembled, rather, the thing the *Times* reporter heard the troops calling it, the *cunt cap* — because upside down it opens to form a rather surprising space with vertical things on each side. Or perhaps the *Times*'s error was the result of some puritan editor ruling, "You can't *say* that!" At any rate, the Army's elite Rangers, traditionally the only wearers of the black beret, were angered by this move to cheapen it and objected to the highest authorities. They won. The whole ordinary Army will not wear the black beret, but will be issued one in a khaki shade. Peace will remain safe.

Uniforms of the Faithful

After looking at so many others, it's a relief to turn for a bit to one large uniformed group refreshingly distant from vanity and mass murder. I'm thinking of the Salvation Army, with its dignified uniforms and modest demeanor.

In America the people of the Salvation Army are most visible ringing their little bells on sidewalks during the holiday season, but in England especially, the "Lassies" of what the British sometimes call the Sally Ann frequent some of the toughest pubs, shaming the drunks, before they take another swallow, into placing on the tambourines some loose change for the poor and hungry. These will be fed and comforted after they have paid the price of listening to a simple, not too long evangelical lecture and some moral exhortation.

The institution was created in 1878 by an English Methodist preacher, William Booth. He was a sidewalk revivalist and conductor of informal missions in London's East End slums. Having observed the ineffectiveness and sloppiness of many social-betterment institutions, he got the idea of starting a more orderly and disciplined evangelical operation, arranged along military lines, with quasi-military uniforms and ranks. This could succeed, we must notice, only at a historical moment when the military could stand as a positive model because it was in relative good odor; Gallipoli and the Battle of the Somme hadn't yet taken place, nor the publicity earned by shocking events in the far future, like the uniformed sadism of the Nazi SS. In England, the Salvation Army seemed a good, almost a noble paradigm of efficient administration and social satisfaction enjoyed by wearers of military uniforms.

Booth's benign militarism expressed itself in the motto "Blood and Fire" on the institution's flag, and his sermons invoked lots of military language, like "this warfare" — that is, between good and evil. Booth's followers were designated "soldiers," and meetings of the leaders became "councils of war." The soldiers even had their own salute, the right-hand index finger pointed "toward heaven."

It cannot be said that taste has ever been among the group's characteristics, but with so much good will, perhaps it's not needed. Today, you're likely to see a soldier of the army in a baseball cap with a red Salvation Army shield on the front, or an officer in full fig, with the ugliest cap device ever invented on the front of his dress visor cap. This device, aping a coat of arms, manages to crowd in as many "symbols" as possible: a five-pointed "crown of life," a capital S worked around a cross, the whole mixture imposed upon crossed swords with "Blood and Fire" surrounding all that, and, below, seven "bullet holes," representing seven verses of Scripture that no one seems to remember very clearly. In case you've missed it, the words "The Salvation Army" at the bottom of the whole presentation explain what you've been puzzling over. In unconscious imitation of Admiral Zumwalt's needless assault upon tradition, the Lassies have forgone their charming straw bonnets in favor of ridiculous, would-be stylish derbys or bowlers, with the SA shield on the front.

Booth devised a set of ranks for those performing administrative or "field" duties. Junior ranks were lieutenant, captain, and ensign. After some months of distinguished service, one ascended to the rank of adjutant, then to commandant, field major, staff captain, brigadier, lieutenant colonel, and colonel. At the top of the hierarchy were lieutenant commissioners and a single commissioner. For himself, Booth reserved the title of general.

The army was musical from the start, emphasizing hymns and simple melodies playable to advantage outdoors at march tempo on brass instruments and bass drum, with additional effects contributed by tambourines. "Onward, Christian Soldiers" (1864) became a staple, and its words were perhaps the trigger of the whole idea in Booth's mind.

The uniforms he invented were of dark blue wool (the Royal Navy influence again?) with a bright red letter S on each lapel of the jacket. Not being in any way a genuine martial institution, the army had no need of a jacket that called exaggerated attention to the wearer's shoulders, although there are understated epaulets, red for officers, blue for others. Dark blue and red were the colors repeated in the Lassies' original bonnets. This headwear was thick and full, stuffed with straw as protection from bricks and similar missiles in the old days of contentious street meetings. "Ridicule and fierce fighting — even to the shedding of blood, was the lot of the first soldiers of the Salvation Army," reports a historian of the organization. Youth who had been drawn to Booth's early meetings were now delighted to have uniforms to wear. "Hitherto," remembered one, "we had worn frock coats and soft hats and carried walking sticks, the latter especially as a means of defense." One can appreciate that Booth's imagery of "army" was not wholly inappropriate.

The army was at the left wing of the theological spectrum. The established church, on the right, was so impressed that in 1882 it invented its own "church army." But radical success was enjoyed by those who came first, with the seasonal tinkling of little bells, the trumpets, tubas, and tambourines, and one of the most dignified uniforms ever worn by any "army."

IF YOU LIKE color on your uniforms, there are three places where you can turn: one is the U.S. Marines in full dress; another is the complete line of uniforms available to the Germans during the Second World War, including the SS; and the third is the Roman Catholic Church and its amazing uniform repertory.

An institution tracing its origins to A.D. 33 or thereabouts can be expected to remember and preserve many of the styles of ancient, medieval, and Renaissance clothing it's been through. Distinctive religious vestments, however, were not worn by the Christian clergy until at least the third century. There was too much persecution of the early church for its leaders to identify themselves, although, in the fourth century, St. Jerome did suggest that priests wear special *clean* clothes when presiding in the sanctuary. But gradually the church moved toward the complex ecclesiastical wardrobe of today, with its numerous quasi-military rules and regulations, mastery of which requires considerable time and effort.

To start with the simplest, most commonly seen uniform: it's the one worn by clerics on the street and is called, officially, *tenue de ville* (called, informally, "clerics"), a suit of black. (Browns, grays, and such are strictly forbidden.) Clerical (or Roman) collar with black dickey or vest with covered buttons, black shoes and socks, of course, and hat and overcoat, if worn, of black too. The Roman collar, by the way, is one of the few items of uniform that does not derive from the deep past; it was invented only in the nineteenth century.

Inside the church or inside its grounds, the priest may wear garments more "historical," notably the floor-length cassock (or soutane) and, on his head, the biretta. With these, symbolism begins to enter. The soutane displays in one long line down the front the most flagrant exhibition of buttons anywhere in the uniform world. There must be thirty-three buttons to symbolize the number of years experienced by the living Christ, while the five buttons on the cuffs are a reminder of the five wounds He suffered at the crucifixion. The collar of the soutane is high but with space in front to allow the white collar to show. Specific rules of rank govern the color of the soutane: for ordinary people, black; for higher ranks, purple; for cardinal, scarlet; and for His Holiness, white. The special soutane allowed only to bishops has a built-in short cape covering the shoulders. For many formal occasions the soutane is worn with the *fascia,* a wide sash, which must also accord with the rank color scheme.

The biretta, a wonderfully archaic stiff square cap, has on top three vanes (or "horns"), together with a tuft. Any devout Catholic is at liberty to relate the three vanes, where one would expect four for symmetry, to the Trinity. One authority on church wear says of the tuft (or "pompon") that it is distinctly "not a tassel and should never appear as one." A thread fastened to the inside of the cap allows the tuft to be made firm by a regulated technique: "when removing the biretta, the center of the frontal horn should be grasped between the index and middle finger." (Military veterans may be reminded of the rhetoric of "training.")

As in the Army, the uniforms get better as you rise in the ranks, and there are plenty of them. At the very bottom, there are monks and nuns and the like, not worthy of serious sartorial mention. Then, ascending, priests and three ranks of monsignors. The rules by which one bishop can outrank another are really too complicated to go into here, although the ranks of cardinals are less threatening: at the top, cardinal bishops; then, coming down, cardinal priests; and, at the bottom, cardinal deacons. Bishops and up are allowed to wear the skullcap, officially called the zucchetto, but only of the right color: for cardinals, scarlet; for bishops, violet; and for the pope, of course, white. Like other holy items, the zucchetto is governed by strict rules. As James Charles Noonan Jr., author and compiler of the invaluable reference book *The Church Visible,* writes, in his effort to enforce correctness, the zuchetto is "never removed at the recitation of the Lord's Prayer as has become the practice of many senior potentates of late. . . . Any prelate choosing to do so, does so solely as a personal gesture and not according to any rubric, law, or long-standing practice."

Throughout the hierarchy, colors have precise meanings, and they must be learned. Red signifies martyrdom; black, humility; and so on, with specific significations for beige, white, yellow, purple, blue, pink, gold, silver, and green. But with all these colors, as with other variables, there are stiff rules to adhere to, providing ample opportunity for pedantry, nitpicking, and, of course, envy. In appraising a photograph of a cardinal, from Chicago, one authority called attention to an unfortunate solecism: "His Eminence incorrectly wears the surplice, as is evident by the full sleeves." Again, only the pontiff is allowed to make use of velvet sandals. One is not to wear a pectoral cross unless he is a bishop, cardinal, or abbot, or, of course, the pope. And it would be embarrassing, or worse, to appear, as a bishop, in the wrong style of mitre; there are three, each appropriate for a certain rank of bishop. In the church, clearly, it is a serious offense to be seen out of uniform, and if we spectators are occasionally amused by all the solemnity about regulations waiting to be broken, a priest is to be admired because he must know them all.

One of the most interesting items of Catholic uniform, interesting because it is minimal and thus refreshingly understated, is the "hospital stole," or mini-stole, which a priest wears when visiting the sick or comforting the injured or dying outdoors. It is a purple ribbon, about an inch and a half wide and a yard and a half long. When it's needed, the priest, in *tenue de ville,* takes it from his pocket, unfolds it, kisses it, says a prayer, and then places it about his neck. He is now prepared, despite his street clothes, to celebrate a sacrament.

Recently, there has developed a movement among the order of Franciscan monks to replace their old uniform with an improved one. The old one is a rough brown robe with a length of rope for a belt. The proposed new one, the brainstorm of a fashion designer in Milan, is of a lighter gray wool and features two front pockets for cell phones and the like. Like Admiral Zumwalt's bright idea, this movement is bound to fail. The whole point of the Franciscan order is not to be up-to-date but to be out of style — that is, virtuous and sensible.

Because for a Catholic cleric following the rules is all-important, as it is in the military, he would do well to place himself in the hands of a reputable clerical supplier. A good one is Martinez and Murphey, who know exactly what one is supposed to wear in any rank or station. This outlet supplies clerical wear to twenty-two hundred priests all over the world, and, as the journalist Barbara Manning reported, Martinez and Murphey "note that when it comes to choosing vestments, clerics can be just as picky and vain as anyone else." They remember "one Catholic priest who objected to a green chasuble because 'it will make me look like an avocado, the way I'm built.'" No wonder the Sally Anns chose to announce their Protestantism by seriously simplifying their *tenue de ville* and making it do for all their occasions.

IF YOU'VE NOT noticed many nuns on the streets lately, the reason may not be that their number has suffered a radical decrease but that they don't all appear in identifiable uniform anymore. A number of nuns, especially those involved in public charitable work, have felt the need to de-uniform themselves, in part to fit more closely into the spirit of reform resulting from Vatican II, and in part to make their job with the often fractious and anticlerical poor easier. Once, the Sisters of Mercy wore the usual black-and-white habit. Now they can wear what they please. Sister Mary Scullion of that community reported that, recently, hoping to refresh her memory, she "went to look for my habit but couldn't find it — I hadn't worn it for so long." These days, as she goes about her daily charitable tasks, she's likely to appear in "normal clothing," like slacks, white blouse, and a cardigan sweater.

Nuns disinclined to appear in the former habit found that looking like a nun was likely to trigger rude reactions, as if the poor were growing snottier or more articulate. Such reactions of course frustrate an order's whole mission of helping the outcast and unfortunate with clothing, housing, food, and courtesy. It shouldn't be overlooked that some hostile reactions to identifiable nuns derive perhaps from memories of needlessly harsh treatment in parochial schools, but the current toughening of attitude may also arise from generalized anger at anything that looks "official." (Still, it's curious that no one seems to mind the Salvation Army members wearing their uniforms.)

Sister Mary noted that the earlier habit distinguished one group of people from others (precisely, one would think, the purpose of a uniform). But, she said, "different periods have different values. Vatican II opened up windows," and today many nuns in the United States do not wear the habit. This is in large part a very American movement, not widespread in Europe. Sister Mary reported that when she was in Rome, she saw black-garbed nuns "all over the place."

"What you wear affects people," she noted. "In today's world religious life strives to be in solidarity with ordinary people. Before, differences in dress tended to suggest separation from people." Homeless people, the special beneficiaries of Sister Mary's labors, "look for caring and acceptance. This is more important than what we're wearing." And Sister Mary is aware of a moral reason not to wear "uniform": even a nun's habit can gratify vanity, the vanity of belonging.

EVERYONE HAS SEEN them, the notably well-behaved groups of young mendicants, heads shaved, and uniformed as if they were sincere, pious citizens of, say, the Republic of India, tinkling their little bells and cymbals while chanting,

> *Hare Krishna, Hare Krishna, Krishna, Krishna,*
>   *Hare, Hare,*
> *Hare Rama, Hare Rama, Rama, Rama, Hare, Hare.*

But for all its air of antiquity and traditionalism, the sect of the Hare Krishna is as deeply an emanation of the American 1960s as Woodstock, bell-bottomed Levi's, and male earrings and necklaces.

Krishna is, of course, the name of a Hindu god, and *hare* is an honorific with various meanings — lord, holy, king, sin-remover. The sect dates from only 1965, when it was founded by A. C. Bhakitivedanta Swami Prabhudpada, a new American immigrant who decided to name his sect the International Society for Krishna Consciousness. Internationally, it's not done very well, and an attempt to install it in India produced annoyance and ridicule. One commentator held that the sect offers a cheerful, joyous approach to the action of finding solace in a mechanistic world. Skeptics may conclude that its optimism is pecularily American and hardly exportable to places with deeper, and nastier, historical experience.

The Hare Krishna uniform involves, first, the *dhoti,* a ceremonial undergarment consisting of cloth wrapped around the waist like a skirt (orange for the celibate, white for the married), pulled up between the legs; and, above, the *kurta,* a long shirt. Also worn are the *tulasi* beads, a simple necklace resembling a rosary. All these (except the beads) must be made from natural fibers, usually cotton, silk, or jute, and the cotton, in deference to the memory of Gandhi, is preferably hand-loomed. Women wear saris, varying in color and design. The lodgement of the sect in the United States produced a tendency for the men to wear, under their *kurtas,* T-shirts with chants inscribed on them.

THERE IS ALWAYS irony in these matters, and one irony here is that the founder, Prabhudpada, chose to wear traditional American garb of the sort worn by not too successful American businessmen. This, together with his temple's location on the inexpensive Lower East Side of New York City, earned him the name of Downtown Swami, in contrast to the Uptown Swami, another Hindu teacher, Swami Nikalananda, who wore a three-piece suit with a pocket watch and catered to the richer people of the Upper East Side. Prabhudpada, who at first imagined that he would attract a highly cultivated, educated audience, was surprised to discover that his early devotees in the New World were kids most kindly designated as dropouts and the usual young desiring to astonish and offend their parents.

THERE IS ANOTHER irony: these young members of the counter-culture, who conceived that by embracing the Hare

Krishna life they were entering an existence unfettered by the rules and codes they were rebelling against, found themselves captives of a severely rigid, demanding system much more given to control than most of the standard religions they were familiar with, all because they had misread the uniform as a celebration of freedom.

WILLIAM DEADWYLER, THE current governing body commissioner of the International Society for Krishna Consciousness, is something of an authority on uniforms. He is the son of an Army officer and the father of a naval one, as well as a deep reader in military history and psychology. He tends to describe secular clothing as "civilian" and even to refer to a secular uniform as "civvies." "I always liked my father best," he says, "when he was in uniform. It was impressive." He fondly recalls the gorgeousness of the old Army pink trousers and deeply regrets their disappearance. Dr. Deadwyler (Ph.D. in religion) has a highly traditional sense of uniforms, noting their "hierarchial" features and their ability to signal status distinctions. "The interesting thing about military uniforms," he points out, "is that you can look at a guy, especially if he's got his dress uniform on and all his medals, and you know everything about him. You have to know the code. Even if you're looking at a civilian, you see how he ties his tie; you can see the cut of his suit." Dr. Deadwyler recalls that in the 1960s, when clergymen were abandoning their uniforms and many their calling, he and other Krishna devotees were busy adopting uniforms. He knew a Catholic priest who discarded his Roman collar in the sixties and wore his hair down to his shoulders, bell-bottomed trousers, and a buckskin jacket with fringe. Both men were astonished to meet and perceive that they had, uniform-wise, changed places. "We had switched uniforms." Dr. Deadwyler is fond of quoting Swami Prabhudpada's response to a reporter who asked why Hare Krishnas dress differently. "It's because we are different," he answered, a useful reminder

of the effect of any uniform, sacred or profane, upon its wearer
and its audience.

SELF-STYLED DRUIDS are another faith-based organization brought into notice by the current leaning toward "spiritu-
ality" attained through association with all-but-forgotten ancient cults and their presumed sages. This phenomenon is
probably best accounted for as a reaction against the gross
materialism and utilitarianism of modern life, a reaction that
sometimes exacts a terrible toll on sensitive minds. But the Druids may have something; in the current atmosphere of intense
ecological consciousness, there are many things you can do to
trees that are worse than worshiping them.

Like similar sects, the Druids are not immune to breaking
up into several quarreling groups, and Druid policy about uniform is at the moment in some disarray. No one quite knows for
sure what the original Celtic practitioners, in Wales and thereabouts, wore, but white or gray gowns are favored by the majority. Some like white for ordinary events but lean to bright
colors for important ceremonies and rituals. Some favor bull
hides, some feathered headdresses. Should female Druids wear
light blue robes? How about speckled and multicolored garments? One spokesman said, "I see no reason why a modern
Druid could not wear a white robe or long shirt with a speckled
or tartan kilt, as part of today's ceremonial garb."

As the question of the color of robes has been fogged by the
continued debate, most Druids seem willing to settle for the
simple white robe as the "official" uniform, especially "when
performing ritual and Druidical actions." This opinion
emerged after decades of amateur historical "research," much
of it really in the service of Welsh or Irish nationalism and self-
respect. We should probably avoid implying any offensive re-
semblances to the original homemade robes of the Ku Klux
Klan, also white because they were fashioned from bed sheets,
pillowcases, and tablecloths. (I might add that the student of

uniform should not waste much time inquiring into the attire of some groups — like Wiccans, believers in benign witchcraft — because most have no regulated dress and, worse, no consistent organization. The investigator will soon find that in these groups most members refuse to recognize any central authority or venerable tradition, indispensable criteria for designating a group *uniformed.*)

TRADITION IS ONE thing no one could accuse the Jewish Hasidim of neglecting. Their name means roughly the Pious, and their movement was founded in Poland around 1750. You see them, especially in New York City, wearing their uniform of beard, black fedora, white shirt without tie, and black, often notably old-fashioned, jacket and trousers. All this is in obedience to Torah, and it exemplifies unambiguously the use of uniforms to establish uniformity — in this case, of thought, feeling, and action.

One highly visible branch of Hasidic Jews is the Lubavitch, whose rabbis and adherents follow a strict dress code, justified by the Talmud. It is a rare element of their uniform that does not carry some religious meaning. For example, they tend to wear clothing made of silk, because on Shabbat (Sabbath), the world is elevated, as Rabbi Levi Haskelevich explained, to a level above presumably insensate things like weeds and stones. Silk, being made by a living creature, attains value because it comes from the highest level of material existence. One could say that there is more of Jehovah in it.

Fixity and stability characterize God's oversight of His creation, and therefore a mode of silent worship is adherence to unchanging tradition, regardless of fashion and changes in the secular world. God has no relation to styles. The Lubavitch adherence to an unchanging uniform has at least two functions: it celebrates the glory of God, and it reminds Lubavitchers of their difference from others, a notable function of all uniforms, civilian and military. The uniform has another meaning, as explained by the rabbi: "Everyone knows that clothing is important, for it represents a significant relationship between man and the material world." Also, "clothing is something which is measured. Too long or too short is not good, not comfortable. You're going to trip on your pants if they are too long. You're going to be cold if they are too short. Clothes that really fit," he said, "give off energy. Godly energy."

Everyone knows that clothing exercises a powerful influence on one's conduct, but the Hasidim take that bromide very seriously, as seen in their attention to the details of the Hasidic uniform, like the wide fur hat and the narrower taller hat. The long black coat, called a *kapota*, is usually made from wool or silk. For prayer, the Hasid wears a length of string as a belt. It's called a *gartel*. The best kind is made of silk. One religious meaning of the *gartel* is that it separates the top of the body (the worthy, the holy part) from the bottom (the mundane, the ordinary), thus adding holiness to the act of prayer.

AND WHAT ABOUT the general rejection of the necktie? For one thing, ties serve no purpose except vanity. For another, they divide the person like the gartel, but in a merely modish way. Again, God has no truck with fashion, and the Hasidim abjure all clothing that leans toward the fashionable. They belong to the service of God, and there's no getting around it.

A SORT OF Protestant Hasidic movement. That might be a not too inaccurate way to describe the beliefs, practices, and uniforms of the Old Order Amish, the curious horse-and-buggy-traveling, exclusivist, black-garbed sectarians of rural Pennsylvania, Ohio, Indiana, and Ontario, Canada.

They arrived in this country in the early eighteenth century, fleeing the corruptions of Europe and drawn by the promise of religious freedom offered by William Penn. The name Amish (they pronounce it *Ah-mish*) derives from Jakob Ammann, an aggressive Swiss bishop of the Reformation. Between sixty thousand and eighty thousand Amish now live near Lancaster,

Pennsylvania, where they pursue quiet family lives and farming — preferring old-fashioned tools and implements and shunning fashionable things like tractors and electricity and motor cars. Their minds are uncluttered by contemporary popular culture, because, having no electricity, they are spared both radio and television. They live a life little different from that of their forebears, and are readily identifiable by their uniforms. Their code of piety and conduct emphasizes everywhere the snares of vanity. Women wear no jewelry and dress in strictly homemade outfits, with long full skirts of solid colors and modest necklines. Aprons: white for the unmarried, black or dark colors for wives. Because they do not cut their hair (a vanity), they wear it pulled back into a bun. They wear no buttons (too modern), relying on pins and snaps.

The men also reject buttons, fastening their lapel-less and pocket-less black jackets with hooks and eyes. Trousers are black, and no zippers are allowed. The trousers of all males are supported loosely by suspenders, belts being thought to tighten trousers too much, risking sexual emphasis. Shoes and socks must be strictly black. The men and boys wear handmade hats with wide brims — straw for summer, black for winter. Since shaving promotes vanity, married men have full beards, but without the usual mustache, omitted because the European soldiers they came to the New World to avoid wore mustaches as a sort of guild signal. The rationale for all this is simple: the Amish serve only God, and, like the Hasidim, they hold that God has nothing to do with fashion or changing styles. The beards, uniform white shirts, and absence of neckties are virtually Hasidic.

To the Amish, God does not require special architecture or the other vanities of churches. Amish worship takes place in the various homes of the faithful, often led not by special clergy but by temporarily elected members of the community. For the Amish, the Bible is literally true, and its injunctions are meant to be obeyed.

Because men and women alike dress uniformly, their regulated clothing makes a powerful statement about the kind of equality pleasing to God. But because they reject birth control and seldom marry outside the sect, the same five family names are found among over 70 percent of the Amish population of Lancaster County. One now and then hears disquieting rumors of six-toed children and similar old-fashioned outcrops of deformities, perhaps not especially gratifying to God.

Deliverers

Next to sailors and marines, perhaps the most enthusiastic devotees of their uniforms are postal workers. The Postal Service's reputation for probity helps assure respect for its uniformed personnel on the street and in stations. As one female letter carrier attested, "Uniform implies that you can be trusted, and so you are treated better." There would seem to be wide agreement that the check proffered by a uniformed postal worker will probably not bounce. The black stripe of the letter carrier's trousers, shorts, and culottes is like that of the military, and it betokens in many ways a similar status. It is strict discipline that helps postal workers, like United States Marines, to keep their honor clean.

For example, a letter carrier finished with his or her daily round may not, in uniform, pause at a bar on the way home. In a T-shirt, OK, but not in the uniform, which the service takes seriously. It provides each employee with an annual uniform allowance amounting to nearly $300, and it is precise in its insistence that only official garb may be worn. This includes shoes and socks. And because so many employees must be outdoors in all kinds of weather, there are official rubber overshoes and official rubber boots as well as twenty different styles of all-weather black shoes and three types of raincoats. Everything worn above the waist bears the postal logo, a stylized eagle's head in blue and white. There are official caps for all purposes and climates: sun helmets (reproductions of solar topees), also useful in the rain, and for hot temperatures there's a mesh model — that's when you wear your Bermuda shorts. There are visor caps for the old-fashioned, but the favorite cap now is the baseball cap, available in two models, one for hot weather, with a mesh back, and one for winter, with a solid back. For really frigid conditions there's a fur cap with ear flaps and a knitted watch cap with a knitted face mask. The service provides weatherproof parkas and windbreakers and heavy sweaters, and it is up-to-date on the facts of life, offering women official postal maternity blouses. Neckties for all are dark blue with tiny red and white dots. All kinds of official gloves can be had: "Sure-Grip," knit, leather with insulated lining, deerskin, and capeskin, and an official black belt too.

Workers indoors have their own uniform items. For men, a cardigan or a sweater vest; for women, dark blue jumper and skirt. For both, official shirts, white with blue pinstripes and long or short sleeves. And for "internal" workers, choice of necktie, either blue or red, with diagonal stripes in postal colors, that is, red or blue. It is clearly a service not at all shy about its patriotism. On each jacket, vest, and windbreaker, there's an inch-wide horizontal stripe in, of course, red, white, and blue. The postal police are vouchsafed their own special uniform, dark blue trousers with light blue stripes, jackets and shirts with shoulder straps and a place for the police badge. And even the vehicle maintenance people have their own outfits, no stripes on the trousers but warm jackets in several styles.

Everything has been so well thought out that even the socks are special. You can wear either postal white or blue, but the white socks (short, usually, but tall also for wear with short pants) have at the top two handsome dark-blue stripes. All these things may be had by mail from numerous approved manufacturers, but post offices in large cities hold occasional uniform fairs, when the manufacturers are invited to lay out their wares and sell on the spot. The whole variety of uniforms reveals remarkable imagination and even taste, and it's not surprising that those who wear them are happy — and trustworthy.

THE THEORY OF uniforms is full of inexplicables, paradoxes, and contradictions. For example, how to reconcile the loathing felt by soldiers for brown uniforms, while dirt- (and even worse-) brown attire seems to delight the employees of the United Parcel Service? And odder still, the UPS uniform doesn't please just UPS males but also hordes of their female customers, throwing them into something like ecstasy.

A United Parcel spokesman explained the color: what is wanted, he said, is a sedate uniform that doesn't show dirt — similar to khaki in the British army, but darker. The company won't allow its deliverers to take their trousers home overnight; they must be washed daily by the company, partly to keep them up to the standard of looking good, but partly to prevent their turning up in the fashion marketplace, where what the journalist Robert Frank calls *delivery chic* becomes more popular daily. Time was when military uniforms, dirty and disused, became all but obligatory among the trendy young. Now it's uniform wear from United Parcel, Federal Express, and — if you can get away with it — the Postal Service itself.

Frank, in the July 1995 issue of *Cosmopolitan,* offered the following potpourri of UPS erotics, disclosing the degree to which "UPS men, the humble couriers in tight brown polyester uniforms driving clunky package trucks, have become sex objects of the service world." It has gone so far that the company has had to turn down "adult" calendar makers who want to depict their drivers as lewd come-ons — although the company doesn't mind if people find its deliverymen cute. (About 93 percent of its deliverers are men.) Sometimes everything matches the dark brown of the uniform, causing one woman to say, "I think I've got a crush on him. He's got brown eyes." Some find even the company's phone number provocative: it's 1-800-PICK-UPS. A teenager recalled how she and a friend would wait at her mother's store every morning at 11:00 for the UPS man — said to be a tan, blond, muscular hunk. "We scheduled our whole morning around it. He looked cool in the uniform and he always rolled his sleeves up so his muscles would show."

And female UPS deliverers have been equally exciting. Patti Anderson, a New Jersey UPS employee, has often been propositioned by dock workers, which, she says, never particularly bothers her. The impression seems to have gone around that there is no such thing as an ugly UPS man or woman. How much of this is evanescent folklore no one will ever know, but it's almost as if a vacuum is being filled and that the UPS deliverer occupies the role once enjoyed by the suburban iceman, who used to deliver great blocks of ice to housewives while the husband was safely out of the way at work. (For more on this subject, see "Erotica and Related Matters," page 186.)

IF YOU LINED up a number of letter carriers, they would resemble the troops of a well-disciplined army. If you lined up a number of Federal Express deliverers, they might remind you of a chorus line in a Broadway musical. Their current get-ups owe as little as possible to the military model, which they used to honor with navy blue trousers and shirts with shoulder strap epaulets.

Their new uniforms were created in 1991 by Stan Herman, the well-known New York fashion designer. They are nothing if not colorful, with emphasis on green, purple, and black in various mixtures. They resemble leisure wear, especially what might be seen at a golf course. Few surprises there, for Herman also designs the uniforms for McDonald's. But he can do the quasi-military look when appropriate, as he has done for Amtrak and both TWA and American Airlines, and he can make single-color outfits attractive as he's done for FedEx's main competitor, United Parcel.

In the Elizabethen period, buffoons wore "motley" — a style of dress featuring tights with legs of different colors. "Motley" would describe the FedEx outfits, likely to present a purple sleeve on a dark blue or black shirt, or one green sleeve on a black or purple shirt. The technique seems to be a way of departing from the symmetry that used to govern livery or the wear of subordinates, like bellboys and doormen. Little of this sort of thing goes on below the FedEx waist; the trousers remain largely black.

The splashes of purple or green make the FedEx employees recognizable, according to Melinda Webber, an authority on uniforms at New York's Fashion Institute of Technology. She pointed out the special difficulty facing contemporary uniform designers for commercial enterprises. The uniforms must keep the wearers happy, proud, and comfortable, with some attention to aesthetics; they must project an unforgettable corporate image to please management; and they must be unique to prevent confusion among customers. What with Newman's rampant purples, greens, and blacks, there's little chance of anyone confusing a FedEx with a United Parcel.

With commercial uniforms developing in the most unlikely places, it's to be expected that more and more elaborate will become the behind-the-scenes trade administration, now the business of the National Association of Uniform Manufacturers and Distributors. It has popularized among its members the high-class euphemism "career apparel." The career apparel trade is doing very well, thank you, because, as the journalist Carina Chocano noted, "Recent decades have seen an explosion in the number of people who wear uniforms to work. An estimated ten percent of the American workforce is required to wear them every day." A tribute to the success of advertising in dominating American life, making mass consumption the only kind that succeeds.

Transportationists

Would you get on an airplane with two pilots who are wearing cut-off jeans?" Although that question was raised by the head of a company that rents pilots' uniforms, its implications are worth attending to.

Once upon a time, a private pilot avid for paying passengers affected a very different sort of uniform from the one stylish at the moment. Roscoe Turner, an aircraft pioneer, chose to appear wearing a pencil-thin mustache and a pseudo-military blue jacket, cavalry twill breeches, and black riding boots. The object was not just to dignify an occupation that otherwise might have seemed too close to the grease-stained mechanic's, but also to remind the pilot himself of the seriousness of the task before him, sharply unlike his feeling when wearing his usual flying suit of ratty old sweater and corduroy trousers.

But if "riding" supplied the would-be analogous classy meaning to early aviation, it was ultimately the United States Navy that came to the rescue of pilots' social identity. Early German dirigibles were referred to as "airships," and the person in command was thus designated "captain" and awarded four gold stripes on his cuffs, just like a real naval captain. His assistant was designated first officer and given three stripes. Reason might have suggested two cuff stripes for the first officer (aka co-pilot) and perhaps a rather thin one for the cabin attendant, recognizing his or her role as something like a chief petty officer's. But, no, the naval captain four-stripe model had to be adopted, presumably to overcome early passengers' terrors and condescension.

One long-time airline pilot commented:

> When aircraft grew from a single open cockpit airplane to one where a co-pilot was added, the airlines were presented with a dilemma. You could no longer refer to the *pilot* (even this name is naval nomenclature) as the person directing the aeroyacht, for there were now two of them up front. Thus a Captain *and* a First Officer would command. Borrowing from the Navy, American Airline's caps were white, and naval officers' stripes were affixed to the sleeves of their blouses. Later, the idiosyncratic influence of the Air Force crept in, and scrambled eggs (actually appropriate lightning bolts shooting out of small puffy clouds) were added to the visor of the Captain's cap, and the Air Force added further influence with the officers' "wings" worn on the left side of the jacket.

The airlines' practice of aping the more familiar world of maritime operation (which, though occasionally hazardous, was not as hazardous as early flying) persuaded Pan American to call its planes "clippers," after the nineteenth-century sailing ships. Pan Am, indeed, was a leader in using pseudo-naval uniforms and adopting naval officers' ranks. On early Pan Am flights the hours were even indicated by ships' bells. Because early passenger flights carried air mail, government regulations required armed protection for them. Thus the pistol pockets sewn into the lining of airline pilots' jackets. Perhaps a bit of the maritime model persists in the cockpit crew welcoming a load of passengers with the salty greeting "Welcome aboard!"

The whole dramaturgy of airline uniforms reveals a lot of its meaning when we invoke more of Erving Goffman's refreshingly comic principles. He noted that most human actions imply a bi-partite context: performance in a front region, populated by an "audience," separate from the rigidity of "backstage," where public eyes and ears are not allowed. In the world of the airlines the front region includes the air terminal and loading gate, where pilots appear with their pseudo-military caps on — and on straight, no levity permitted — and the passenger cabin of the plane itself. There is hardly a repeated human action anywhere faster than the speed with which pilot and co-pilot, safely installed in their backstage cockpit with the door closed, safely whip off jackets, caps, and neckties, and every element of their front-region appearance they can jettison to prepare for reality. One former pilot recalled flying as first officer with a pilot given to satirizing the romantic pretensions of the uniform by putting on, once the door was closed, a down-to-earth railway engineer's blue-striped cap.

There was much uncertainty at first about what stewardesses should wear and what they should be called. At first they were dressed as domestic maids, nurses, and even chorus girls. Originally, some airlines called them hostesses, but the grand term flight attendants has apparently won. (Cynics can be heard speaking of them, but never, of course, to their faces, as waitresses.) Male flight attendants are officially (the naval influence once again) stewards, sometimes known unofficially and cruelly as astrofags.

The problem of what to dress women in when, as pilots, they appear in the front region has been solved by the usual approach of simply varying physiologically the dominating male's uniform. At first, female pilots were given trousers insufficiently cut to female proportions. Then dark skirts with an altered jacket to accommodate what used to be called the bust. One woman pilot, not in commercial service but in the RAF, said to her fellow airwomen, "Think yourself lucky you're not in the RAF. Under the flying suits styled only for men, we are supposed to be wearing Y-front long johns."

Why pilots wear uniforms at all has interested one participant in the *Pilots' Rumor Network,* an Internet facility full of good things:

> I suppose that historically uniforms came from the nautical/military connections, but that all seems somewhat dis-

tant and irrelevant now. Why not just wear comfortable clothes? Does anyone know of any research which finds passengers are comforted by uniforms, gold bars, caps, etc., or do uniforms say more about pilots' perceptions of themselves?

In view of September 11, 2001, little research will be needed to emphasize the dramaturgic usefulness of aircrew uniforms, especially those of pilot and co-pilot. The more they resemble military and police personnel, and of the toughest and most disciplined kind, the better. It might not be going too far to propose their bearing conspicuous sidearms, together with handcuffs and containers of Mace and pepper spray.

READERS NOT QUITE born yesterday will recall Glenn Miller's "Chattanooga Choo-Choo," popular in the 1940s, when numerous, apparently thriving railways crisscrossd the United States and when travel by propeller-driven aircraft was rare, utilized by the rich or the famous — or the exceptionally brave. In those days, train conductors were conspicuous, no matter how shiny their navy blue uniforms, for their brass buttons and unusual kepi-style caps. Few young boys would want to be "po'tuhs" or conductors today, when the buttons are a cheap-looking silver color, and the navy blue has given way to a kind of show-business light bluish-gray. A certain amount of a conductor's seriousness seems to have been lost, together with the old uniform that helped sustain it. With its brass buttons, it presented a powerful image of authority. In the old days, conductors had to be prepared to expel from the train difficult drunks, fare dodgers, fistfighters, proven card cheats, and the like. Now, if we consider what the new uniform says, Amtrak conductors are expected to radiate only friendliness and good will. And an up-to-date fashion sense, provided by Stan Herman in league with the United States Government.

The new high-speed train service, designated Acela, has occasioned the revolutionary new uniforms for all personnel, porters, food-service people, ticket sellers — the lot. It would have been easy and less expensive for Amtrak to copy some of the old uniforms, but now, when the "new" and the "novel" must be invoked to propel every commercial phenomenon, we are informed that "the new Amtrak uniforms were created by acclaimed fashion designer Stan Herman, whose impressive array of clients already included Federal Express, McDonald's, Parker Meridien Hotel," and so on. A poster promises "World Class Uniforms for World Class Employees."

Amtrak conductors hoped that the new, no matter what it looked like, would be an improvement in many ways over the old, for in the former uniform, the jacket lining ripped often. And the old uniform, authoritative as it may have been, was designed without a pocket deep enough to hold the conductor's book and stuff. "When you bent over," one conductor testified, "they'd fall out of your pockets," and all the pockets were easily torn or came unsewn. Clearly, a replacement was in order, and here it was, suggesting not just new uniforms but a whole new world:

FOR IMMEDIATE RELEASE
AMTRAK MAKES A FASHION STATEMENT, UNVEILS
NEW EMPLOYEE UNIFORMS

Amtrak employees today [October 20, 1999] staged a fashion show to display the new uniforms that conductors, ticket agents, Red Caps and other workers will begin wearing systemwide. . . . The new uniforms . . . are the result of extensive input from Amtrak employees and customers . . . Amtrak selected the Stan Herman studios . . . from several nationally known design houses. A three-time Coty Award winner . . . Herman met personally with employees to get a true sense of their needs and preferences. . . .

Of course, this doesn't mean that conductors' books won't continue to fall to the floor during the great new twenty-first century. Told that many passengers like the new uniforms, one conductor (age, about fifty-five) said, with some vehemence, "We don't. The cloth is too thin, and the jacket's going to wear out fast. I liked the old suit much better."

The old suit, conceived well before the invention of the zipper, exhibited many brass buttons, for conductors wore vests in addition to their jackets. Since in those days gentlemen generally wore vests with their suits, the vest helped raise the status of the conductor, especially when it allowed him to present a row of at least twelve brass buttons.

But something of the aura of the old conductor's uniform is still available to the minor, harmless weirdos who buy conductors' outfits on the Internet. These folks call themselves "collectors," and they must enjoy the fantasies of power brought them by wearing the uniform. You can order from the Internet not just the uniform, with its plethora of brass buttons, but a conductor's punch for canceling "tickets." You need not be satisfied with a punch that is common and standard, leaving a mere hole in the ticket. For an extra price you can acquire a special punch with a unique die (your initials, etc.). And the purchaser is urged to "add to your professional appearance" by investing in various cap badges and even an authoritative ticket-punch leather holster. Remember those chrome-plated coin holders and change-makers worn on the belt? You can get one of them, too, and play conductor whenever the mood strikes.

The Pullman porters idolized by Booth Tarkington's Herman had less opportunity for wielding power than did conductors, but they had some. By delaying making up a passenger's berth, a porter could exercise a bit of control and thus earn some dignity. Stan Herman, advertising, publicity, and show business have put a stop to all that.

ONE SOCIAL DISTINCTION not widely known is important to a lot of people. It lies in the difference between two types of bus drivers, urban versus long distance. Long-distance drivers (they like to call themselves motorcoach operators) must be more talented than the Ralph Kramden sort, who ply the same route daily. Motorcoach operators have to know the whole country, or at least wide areas of it, and their importance is like railway conductors', because they must stay on schedule, keep order among the equivalent of a railway car's number of people, and, for the sake of their riders' morale, behave as if every annoyance can be easily overcome. Clearly, special dignity and authority are required, but they must not compromise an impression of friendliness. The driver's uniform makes a significant contribution to this whole presentation, and if it is nice enough, the uniform will convey an air of friendliness, too.

The motorcoach operator, indeed, has in some respects a harder role to play than the railway conductor or even the airline pilot, for there is no first officer or other uniformed subordinate to help out, nor has he or she a backstage area for occasional refuge. And, like a railway conductor, the operator needs a degree of acting ability to avoid giving the impression of having favorites among the passengers or being unable to cope with emergencies.

Ephrata, Pennsylvania, is the headquarters of the Elite Coach Company, and one of its drivers, Jim Garman, agreed to be our amiable authority.

"T-shirts have no place in driving a bus," he explains, because greater dignity is required in handling local and long-distance charters as well as custom-group tour planning. Dignity is supplied by the uniform provided by the company: gray trousers, conservative leather shoes, white shirt, burgundy necktie. "We feel," says Jim, "that the uniform goes with the profession." Jim's passengers, he tells us, are an upscale group — doctors, lawyers, bankers — and the assumed high expectations of such people are what Elite proposes to satisfy. A bus driver just drives a bus, but a motorcoach operator "takes care of his people." Such care is visible primarily in little details, and the customer can't help thinking that, for example, a properly uniformed person is "someone I'd like to drive with."

To Jim's intense disapproval, some companies allow their drivers to wear blue shirts and baseball caps, and, even worse, permit them to wear the shirts unbuttoned at the collar. A bad practice, Jim emphasizes, because in our society a white shirt, even without a tie, is "synonymous with class." That he is a professional is important to Jim Garman, and as such he recognizes the importance of self-discipline. And other kinds too, for he was raised in the days of the hickory stick and the leather strap. "Violent people" lack discipline, and, while talking with him, one suspects that he'd like to see everyone in America wearing uniforms, or at least compulsory white shirts. The pride he takes in doing his job well cannot be missed. He speaks proudly of how important it is for him to get his bus as close as possible to the door of a restaurant, museum, or point of tourist interest, to help the elderly off the bus, and to make all his passengers feel comfortable. His satisfaction with his uniform, especially the white shirt and necktie, is a help.

Police and Their Impersonators

When I began working on this book, one question I hoped to answer was why Anglo-Saxon police uniforms are dark blue. Why not green or red, or, less implausibly, brown or khaki? Now I think I've found part of the answer.

When urban police started the dark blue tradition in the middle of the nineteenth century, they wanted to imitate uniforms already familiar to the populace and suggestive of authority, efficiency, courage, and general unbribability. As models, they had available their countries' armies, but because both British and American armies needed uniforms for people fighting on the ground, they favored earth colors for camouflage. The police clearly had no need for camouflage; just the opposite. So there remained the model of the navy, and navy blue became the color for the police uniform to imitate. Thus, the police avoided looking like civic Brown Jobs, with the concomitant social debasement. But even with that conclusion understood and accepted, a question still remains: Why did navies choose dark blue in the first place?

Until the early twentieth century it would have been hard to distinguish American urban police from British, for both wore the kind of helmets (dark blue or gray) still be to seen in London. And not just helmets but luxuriant mustaches. In both places, the high-collared jackets were long, almost to the knees, and were decorated with two grand rows of brass buttons, sixteen in all. (This was precisely the uniform of the Keystone Kops.) Personnel above the rank of patrolman or constable wore visor caps, but it was left to the Americans to devise the familiar visored police cap worn by all ranks, called in the trade an eight-pointer, designating the points around the crown. In many police forces dark blue conveys honorific meaning by itself, because probationary officers wear gray uniforms, ascending to blue only after considerable training and experience. Officers promoted from the one status to the other are described as "moving up to the blue." The whole outfit is often referred to not as the Blue but as the Bag. Despite the rejection of the army model for color, most police forces use army insignia to indicate grades: sleeve chevrons for patrolmen, metal shoulder or collar insignia for the higher ranks. One even sees police chiefs wearing the four silver stars of full general, and lesser officers wear the gold and silver bars of army lieutenants and captains. State police, whose venue is the outdoors, especially the highways, tend toward khaki or gray uniforms, with the wide-brimmed Stetson hat, and some state police forces have their right to wear that hat protected by law.

The advent of female uniformed police has, of course, required a certain amount of give in the specifications, but there is a current loosening of uniform regulations for all, like the use of the dark blue golf jacket and the novelty of sweaters, including turtlenecks in both white and black, with the white allowed only to lieutenants and above. And the institution of police on bicycles has made the hideous bike helmet standard, which has badly lowered any pretensions to dignity that might remain.

Now, a bit of sartorial conservatism. Some people are unable to resist the impulse to improve what is familiar and perfectly satisfactory. Admiral Zumwalt was one, and, as we shall soon see, Richard Nixon was another. So was the anonymous but despicable contriver of the beret as a replacement for the academic mortarboard. A psychologist at Stanford University wondered whether the police might be more loved if they wore something other than the traditional dark blue outfit. Maybe things would go better if the police appeared in the outfit ("uniform"?) preferred by servicemen when not uniformed — gray or khaki slacks with navy blue blazer. He thought the omission of pistols and nightsticks would be an improvement, too.

What he found surprised him. He discovered that the standard dark blue uniform is joyously received by most citizens, and that officers in traditional dress are perceived as possessing better judgment and as being more competent, helpful, honest, fast, and active than those in "modern" uniforms, comprising slacks and blazers. In addition, what police officer would not feel naked and powerless without "the belt," supporting pistol holster, handcuffs, nightstick, and traffic-ticket book? It can be added that since both airplane pilots and police forces have gone to the look of naval officers for their inspiration about uniforms, it seems little wonder that, despite the new green uniforms, the army nurtures secret feelings of being second-rate and no 'count.

An added police duty is keeping an eye on the uniformed security guards employed by stores to discourage shoplifting. The real police must make sure that the security guards' uniforms are not — as the stores hope they will be — easily confused with actual police garb. Some commercial guards hope to resemble police by carrying their cell phones in black leather holsters, just as if they were pistols.

Another threat to the uniqueness of police appearance comes from companies supplying uniformed strikebreakers (excuse the expression). These wear two grades of attire, designated low profile and high profile. The low-profile uniform consists of green or blue trousers, white or dark blue shirt with pseudo-police badge, and baseball cap. The high profile outfit closely resembles the kind associated with a SWAT team or military unit — battle dress with badge. If you run a strike-menaced company, you can also hire a unit equipped with cameras for use in later prosecution, or in present coercion. In offering its services to companies expecting or experiencing a strike, the Special Response Corporation of Baltimore (that's the one I'm talking about) provides, in addition to quasi-authoritative uniforms, researched material for use in legal arguments, threats, or blackmail. And you can purchase a whole documentary package, which will give you data on the salaries of fourteen national labor union leaders.

The logo of the Special Response Corporation depicts both an American eagle and the American flag. Elderly people whose memories are as yet undamaged will easily imagine that they are back in the union-busting 1930s, when strikes were conventionally depicted as unpatriotic and when physical strikebreakers and scabs were plenteous. But then corporations had to supply such people from less commercial sources. Then, there were no police impersonators to do the job for them.

Why Aren't Grave Violations of Taste
Impeachable Offenses, Too?

Elmo Zumwalt is not the only public person to stumble over a question of uniforms. Another famous man also had naval experience, but way back in the Second World War, where he apparently devoted more time to playing poker than to destroying his country's enemies.

I speak of Richard Nixon, the awkward and angry sad sack from nondescript Whittier, California. In 1970, he had just returned from some state visits in Europe, and he couldn't get over the various colorful guards who had performed in his honor and stood at attention while he inspected them. They wore grandiose uniforms. The president was so impressed by things like large bearskin shakos and bright red jackets that he forgot that these countries were largely monarchies reduced now to pseudo-monarchies, while his own country was based in part on its official hostility to any kind of royalty or peerage.

Afire with memories of the way he'd been honored by flashy uniforms all over the place, he wondered why his country couldn't honor him in the same way.

To this end, he consulted the District of Columbia's pre-eminent uniform specialist, one Jamie Muscatello, who once ran a uniform factory specializing in sailors' wear. Later, he branched out into police uniforms, and if you happened to be chief of staff of one of the armed services, you probably had Jamie measure you and make you a fine outfit. It is said that it was Jamie Muscatello who helped the White House select a more impressive uniform for the White House police, formerly dressed in normal police uniforms, with the occasional white shirt instead of dark blue. Jamie brought a selection of samples to the White House for the scrutiny of Mr. H. R. Haldeman, Mr. John D. Ehrlichman, and the boss himself. They agreed on a new uniform and ordered a hundred and fifty outfits.

The White House police wore them for the first time to grace a visit by British Prime Minister Harold Wilson. The president, who said at the time that he wanted to add to the dignity of White House affairs, expected these uniforms to inspire awe and respect. What he got — and the response could have been predicted by any half-bright citizen — was a cascade of ridicule and abuse.

The new uniforms are hard to describe without laughing. First, the hat: a black plastic semi-shako with visor. It rose a full seven inches, and Washington hadn't seen its like since the British and Germans fought us in the 1770s. Then, there was the tunic: high-collared, cream-colored, double-breasted, with a heavy gold fourragère (one of those fancy cords worn around shoulder and armpit) hanging from the right shoulder. Belt and pistol holsters were of shiny black, apparently "patent" leather. Each side of the old-fashioned high-buttoned collar bore the initials WH so that there would be no uncertainty over whom these preposterous cops belonged to.

Those who tried to keep straight faces may have recalled Kingsley Amis's observation that "the funniest thing in the world is solemnity." "Fancy attire" sneered *U.S. News & World Report*. Other media alluded to Ruritania and comic opera. Those with theatrical memories pointed to the pretentious uniform worn by Prince Danilo in *The Merry Widow* and the uniforms in the light operas of Sigmund Romberg. There was hardly anyone who didn't find it all very Balkan and much more suitable for a bad monarchy than a good republic.

And what happened to these costly hundred and fifty uniforms? No one is quite sure or willing to talk, but the highly credible rumor is that they became the property of a high school band in Iowa. Worth noting is the approximate simultaneity of Zumwalt's uniform initiative and Nixon's bright idea, which a year later triggered memorable mimicry by Philip Roth in *Our Gang*. It is no surprise to hear Jamie Muscatello asserting that the president "saved all his letters from people praising his efforts on the uniform."

Youth on the Musical March

If Richard Nixon's comical White House police uniforms did end up bringing a touch of tacky grandeur to a high school band in Iowa, that would suggest the style to which such bands aspire. Dignity is not wanted, nor is humor. Flashiness is. Shakos with erect plumes are in great demand, as are capes, epaulets, white gloves, even white spats. Many students adept at clarinet or trombone are enticed to join the band by the uniform alone.

The world of high school marching bands is not well known, except to state and county purchasing agents, for whom it is very big business, like *The Music Man* multiplied a hundredfold. In the state of Pennsylvania alone there are nearly seventy-five high school marching bands, with about a hundred kids per band, to be purchased for, fitted, and sartorially instructed. Local pride is at issue, and appearance and the expenditure necessary to sustain it are not to be compromised. The adult leaders of the band, perhaps on tenure, must be adept at teaching not just instrumental music but mass choreography, the technique of the knee-high strut and the quick march to speeded-up tempos, as well as the psychology and philosophy of absolutely straight lines. He (very seldom she) must double as a drill sergeant, but a likeable one, and his product, when in motion, must look, in Kurt Vonnegut's words, "like a block of postage stamps." There's nothing like uniforms worn early in life to instill uniformity. If you want anything like individualism, go somewhere else.

The degree to which quasi-military uniformity and discipline are required is known largely to participants and their families, and most of the student musicians like it that way. Here's a selection of the rules governing one Midwestern high school band.

What You Should Have:

1. Band Baseball Cap
2. Band Bag
3. Shako Hat Box, Plume
4. Band T-shirt
5. Uniform Coat and Pants
6. Black Socks (Extra Pair)
7. White Drillmaster Marching Shoes
8. White Gloves (Extra Pair)
9. Music Lyre (Wind Players)
10. Band Raincoat
11. Band Garment Bag and Plastic or Wooden Hanger

Top to Bottom:

The Hat Is Called a Shako.
1. Long hair is neatly arranged so that it fits up inside the shako.
2. The brim of the hat is level at the eyebrows.
3. The chin strap should rest on the chin or under the chin.
4. The plume is straight.

The Coat:
1. You should have a sweat-collar snapped inside the coat neck. The neck collar is hooked shut.
2. If your coat fits properly your sleeves should touch the wrist area of your gloves when your instrument is up and you

should have room to breathe. You should not be able to see the side adjustment zippers on your pants if your coat fits properly.

3. You should always wear a band shirt or white T-shirt/sweatshirt, sweater, or long underwear under your coat. Sleeveless tops, tank tops, or colorful shirts are not permitted. Sleeveless shirts allow underarm stains to occur on the coat. Colorful shirts often fade when you sweat or get wet. Colorful shirts can often be seen through the white portions of the uniform.

The Pants:

1. The pants should fit high up on the chest. They should be adjusted so that the bottoms of the pants touch the tops of the shoes and are approximately one inch from the ground. They should not drag on the ground.
2. The sides adjust with zippers and the length can be adjusted with the suspenders.
3. You may wear shorts, long underwear, jeans, sweats, etc., under your pants but they should not be visible at all when you move, stand still, or mark time.

Gloves:

1. All sections wear white gloves except the percussion section. You must provide your own white gloves.
2. Flutes, clarinets, and saxes may choose to cut the fingers out on the palm side of the gloves for keys that require coverage. Do not cut the fingers tops off the gloves.
3. Gloves should always be clean before a performance.

Care Tips:

Hat: you should wipe the inside and the outside of the hat often with a damp cloth, using a mild soap. Be sure to dry with a soft cloth and air out the hat before you put it away. Sweat can make your hat smell very bad. Plumes should be kept in the plume case. . . . Be sure you have a plastic bag for a plume cover.

Uniform Coat and Pants: You can brush dirt from your uniform with a garment brush. Do this after every performance. The band will dry clean the uniforms twice during the year. . . . Do not attempt to repair the uniform yourself. Do not wash or dry clean your uniform on your own.

General Information:

You are not permitted to wear jewelry from the neck up or if it is visible on any other body part when in uniform. . . . Nail polish should be removed if you do not wear gloves or if it will be visible at any time when in uniform.

(All, perfect preparation for a career in the Marine Corps.) You would find roughly the same injunctions issued to university band members, although the older and, in their view, more sophisticated universities allow some leeway. The height of sophistication among university marching bands of the Ivy League is to choose as a uniform what an idle rich boy or girl would have worn at a summer outing about 1908: a straw boater, white sweater with institutional initial in block letters, white flannel trousers or skirt, sometimes navy blue blazer. White shoes looking like buckskin but secretly cleated to avoid slippage on damp grass. The ideal tone is understatement, with archaic touches. For example, the straw boaters, suggestive of antiquity and solidity, as well as privileged British overtones.

The band of the University of Pennsylvania is typical in following the laid-back style of the Ivy League. Regarding marching as a high school occupation and puerile, it describes itself as a "scramble" band. Members enter the playing field in conspicuous, careless disorder, like thoroughly drunken and aimless children of the upper class. Suddenly, to the presumed surprise and delight of the audience, they scramble into their assigned places and form up as if they'd formally marched in. Among the Ivy, Cornell is the only institution to stick with the style of the pseudo-military marching band, with uniforms to match, little different from those worn in high school. The Penn (and standard Ivy) uniform includes white gym shoes, white socks, khaki trousers, white shirts with collar, and navy blue sweater with red and blue block "P." "No hats, no feathers" is the way one member describes the style. The band used to wear white trousers but found them "too uniformish" and replaced them with khakis like those students might wear to class.

One Penn band member liked this informal style but was generous enough to admit admiring the formal style exemplified by the band of the University of Michigan. "They practice every day. They start before school begins. They are excellent, excellent, excellent. I absolutely admire them. If I went to that school, I would do that." But, she concluded, "we are different. If you wanted to have a precision marching band, you couldn't wear these Penn clothes. Since we just run around the field screaming, we get to wear sweaters."

Another member of the Penn band prefers the informal because it is less embarrassing than the "military" when you're alone, perhaps some distance from college. "If you're walking by yourself in full uniform, you really stand out." (Nice understatement there.) One can perhaps understand that students at recently founded universities without much prestige want to be conspicuous, while others like the understated style. But there's always the Ivy student unable to forget or patronize the exciting discipline and looks of the band at the University of Michigan.

Doorpersons, etc.

Although the time-honored term "doormen" may be invoked without blame (I've never seen a female one), it would be a mistake to call doormen's outfits "uniforms," for they are generally worn by only one person, and large groups of doormen identically clad are seldom seen. But whether worn outside a hotel, theater, or expensive restaurant, the get-ups of these people look like uniforms, and that may be sufficient reason for including them. And they may actually be conceived as vaguely military, for in England, at least, many doormen are by tradition retired old soldiers who still like to look trim and proud.

Robert S. Ames, a former airline pilot, and thus familiar with proper standards among the uniformed, reports that a young Canadian doorman he witnessed was "a disgrace to the uniform. It's much too large, and the cap is about to blind him." Formerly, Ames correctly notes,

> the doormen were almost always veterans of various wars of the Empire; their uniforms were of perfect fit, and they also wore their ribbons of campaigns and heroism on their doormen's uniform. Today the doormen are not venerable and admirable but jobless youths who might just as well be waiting in restaurants or slinging hash at a McDonald's. These young doormen do not, of course, regard what they're doing as a lifetime profession. Just a job. And their uniform is likely to be a one-size-fits-all affair, kept in

a back closet and worn with high embarrassment. Individual uniforms that fit are an expense that hotel managements no longer wish to endure.

When standing at the entrance to a hotel or posh apartment house, ideally the doorman serves as living advertising — of the class and grandeur of what's inside the building. Hence a real doorman's devotion to lots of brass buttons. Robert Benchley is said to have come out of the door of a Manhattan restaurant and asked a uniformed man at the door, "Would you get me a taxi, please?" "I'm sorry," the man replied, "I'm an admiral in the United States Navy." (That playlet would have occasioned ample amusement, with no need for the customary final line, which moved Benchley into an easy and rather vulgar comic tradition quite foreign to him: "All right, then get me a battleship.")

Regardless, "admiral" is a favorite model for the doorman's uniform: navy blue, with stripes down trouser seams, long pseudo-frock coat, with copious brass buttons. Gold stripes, of course, around the cuffs. It's all self-explanatory: with an admiral at the entrance, you are not likely to brush shoulders with prostitutes and thieves. A recent book for children, Edward Grimm's *The Doorman*, gets it right. The apartment house doorman in question is exemplary: "He felt responsible for everyone who lived there — as if he were the captain of a ship."

Upper Fifth Avenue in New York is where you can behold some of the best doormen. In addition to admiral, another favorite model is czarist general about 1914, before the Revolution put everyone, high or low, into either rags or ill-fitting "business" suits. Both admiral and general elevate the imagery of servanthood, unlike one doorman who works at an urban hotel dressed up horsy to look like a groom, boots and all, as if just emerging from his smelly stable chores.

Parents in New York know how indispensable doormen are when their children have to walk to school. Uniformed doormen, they know, function as surrogate police. One observer notes, "Children traveling to and from school have been urged to notice the apartment buildings along their route which have uniformed doormen who can serve as protectors in time of danger." It's the uniform of high rank that makes the difference. You can't be of service that way if you look like a mere groom.

There is another uniformed group indispensable in classy accommodation institutions: the corps of bellhops — or bellboys, no matter their age. Their most natural habitat is hotels, but until the Atlantic was no longer crisscrossed by luxury liners, they performed on shipboard as well. Indeed, a favorite publicity photo enticing well-to-do prospects to sail on a certain ship was a picture of that vessel's bellboys having their fingernails inspected for cleanliness in a pseudo-military way by a ship's officer. The normal corps of bellboys numbered about twenty, but on extravagantly grand ships, it was much larger. The *Normandie* had eighty bellboys, ready to deliver letters and notes, flowers, bottles, and boxes of candy in return for generous tips.

The standard bellboy uniform was the same on sea or land, and it is stamped forever on the public mind by the cigarette ads of the 1940s featuring "Johnny," the small boylike man repeating his "Call for Philip Morris" while presumably paging the guest of some grand hotel or ship. He wore the classic uniform: black trousers with broad red stripes, high-collared waist-length red jacket (in British, *bum-freezer*) with a total of twenty brass buttons, white gloves, and, tellingly, the red pillbox cap mock impudently tipped far to one side of his head.

This was the outfit worn by seventeen-year-old Clyde Griffiths in Theodore Dreiser's *An American Tragedy,* when he was lucky enough to find work as a bellhop in one of Kansas City's finest hotels. Far from feeling in any way humiliated by the uniform, he was proud of it, for it signaled that he was definitely not one of the shiftless but was indeed tightly disciplined, ready to jump to it at any moment when called. His uniform belonged to the hotel, and he got to wear it free. It was maroon, "bright with many brass buttons," and, for his head, "a small, round pillbox cap . . . cocked jauntily over one ear." When, starting out, he was taken to the hotel's wardrobe department, he was fitted with a uniform requiring no alteration at all. The perfect employee. Clyde, accustomed to severe poverty, was ecstatic: "He was to be a bellboy in the great Hotel Green-Davidson. He was to wear a uniform and a handsome one." The vanity of belonging could hardly have had a more telling moment.

Despite some appearances and some folklore, the same vanity applies to waitresses and waiters privileged to appear in their employers' uniforms. For waitresses of the past, these uniforms didn't deviate very far from black dresses with white collars and cuffs, and, very often, white aprons. If the apron was by design tiny and flirtatious, it assisted the effect of the white cap worn well back on the head. Seldom seen today, this outfit was largely ousted by the startling mode, like the one on show in a successful "diner style" restaurant in a large city. There, waitresses wear a uniform of blue denim bib overalls with a white collarless shirt, on one of whose short sleeves appears the restaurant's logo. One representative waitress is very happy with this uniform, saying of the shirt especially, "It's roomy, it's spacious, and it's comfortable for the kind of work we're in." She likes the bib overalls because they have "loads of pockets for pens and books and people's money." Like most uniform wearers, she appreciates the convenience of not having to pick out her clothes in the morning. "I don't have to wake up every morning and try to figure out what I'm going to wear for that day at work." (That could be said by most people, employed or not. Everyone has a uniform and if possible wears it every day, except, perhaps, Sundays and other special days. Saves thinking and the work of remaking one's external character all the time.)

That waitress's boss chose these bucolic uniforms because they convey, he says, a wholesome, rural image, and the waitresses like them because they save wear and tear on their own clothes, which some restaurants require them to wear with only the business's apron to signal their position.

Although it may be a mistake to designate the employees in a McDonald's "waitresses" and "waiters," they have recently been dolled up by the ubiquitous Stan Herman. The employees, say the management, are mostly young and "have to look friendly and hip." One way to convey that impression is to get rid of all neckties and to provide a zippered vest to go over a short-sleeved shirt. All in two shades of dark blue with gold facings on the collar to remind viewers of the trademark arch. Trousers are black. They don't matter much, for their wearers are almost always behind a counter.

LIKE MOST LARGE hotels in self-important cities like New York, the Plaza takes uniforms very seriously. It has a non-publicized wardrobe department to outfit its one thousand employees. Mr. Will Eye, the director of this operation, explained why waiters and busboys must not be dressed in any way alike. Waiters wear white jackets; busboys, black. "When you have these big functions, you don't want the guests going to a busboy, so you dress them differently, and the one that looks better is the one you want people to speak to." (Does this imply that the Plaza carefully hires ugly busboys?) Mr. Eye is also in charge of chefs' outfits and, as a functionary of a grand hotel, is vigorously opposed to novel dress by the kitchen staff. He says, "You've got to be professional. Just imagine a chef with no hat. First of all, it's a state law that you've got to wear a hat." He feels strongly that the baseball caps allowed in inferior hotels must never appear in the kitchens of the Plaza, even if no one is looking. "Baseball caps are unprofessional. That is — you've got to understand — this is the Plaza Hotel. Movies are made here. It has a reputation worldwide. You don't see us advertise in the newspaper, like Marriott or someplace like that." The employees easily take on Mr. Eye's pride in being associated with such an institution, suggesting why the United States Marines so seldom lack for recruits.

The Pitiable Misfits of the Klan

The loosely organized groups identifying themselves as elements of the Ku Klux Klan have so long been the targets of legal action and public contempt that they do not give out information readily. But in the search for the rationale of their uniforms, one can come up with some meager stuff. The problem is that the Klan as an organized national group cannot be said to exist; decades of internecine quarrels have broken it into a number of feeble local simulacra, which spend a lot of time traducing one another.

It all began well over a century ago as an effort to scare Southern former slaves after the Civil War. The first Klan is said to have been organized in Pulaski, Tennessee, in 1866. The hope was to frighten Negroes into accepting the white-sheeted figures on black horses as the ghosts of Confederate soldiers killed at Shiloh or Bull Run and now enacting their disapproval of Reconstruction. Beginning as a cruel practical joke, these nocturnal visits to black premises evolved into a device of coercion, and finally as a technique of local lynching difficult to prove because of the number of attackers and their masks. By the 1920s the movement had spread to the Middle West. It enjoyed great success in Indianapolis, which in 1910 had the largest black population of any city north of the Ohio River, and, before long, Klan groups committed outrages all over the North. Unable to unify, they remained local and simply made up names for themselves. We hear of the White Knights of [insert name of State], the Knights of the White Kamellia, the Invisible Circle, the Knights of the Southern Cross, and so on. Anyone could organize a unit of the Klan without guidance. One failed attempt to unify the groups is that of the United Klans of America, Inc., based in Tuscaloosa, Alabama. It supplies an order form for its robes and regalia, but its purpose is clearly less political and criminal than commercial.

The robes and masks worn at occasional cross burnings and similar local ceremonies are white less for a symbolic reason (like "For Whites Only") than because white was the color of the bed sheets, pillowcases, and tablecloths constituting the original ad hoc disguises.

Anyone asking, "Yes, but where do these robes and pointy hoods with eyeholes come from today?" may be instructed by the example of forty-seven-year-old Janet Williams (not her real name), who lives in Goshen, Indiana. She runs up Klan uniforms on her home sewing machine, filling orders privately. She reports that she clears about sixty dollars on each robe and hood, and says, "I guess I'm one of three or four people in the nation who makes robes and hoods." She's a devotee of words like "nigger," "kike," and "spic," and, afraid of her neighbors' assumed ill-will, she keeps loaded firearms in her house. She is an ordained minister of the Universal Life Church of California (where else?). You can learn about her on the Internet, sub voce *klan*.

Some Klannish groups occasionally appear in a more conventional uniform than white robe and hood. It's worn largely by young men on recruiting duty at carnivals, state fairs, and the like. It consists of a white shirt with black necktie. On the upper right sleeve, a patch depicting the United States flag. On the left, the Confederate flag. On the left side of the shirt, an emblem of the Christian cross and a large stylized blood drop. On the right, a black-and-white crosswheel. The baseball cap reads Knights of the Ku Klux Klan, with a smaller blood-drop-over-cross emblem. The number and quality of rubes attracted by the display of this odd outfit is not known.

Of course, the Klan spirit will never be entirely obsolete, for the supply of what the attorney general of Alabama has called "pitiable misfits" has no limit.

Unbelievable as it may sound, there have always been some Klansmen who conceive that the Klan has never gone far enough in dealing with its enemies. Some of these people spun off in the 1920s to form the Black Legion, and they adopted a uniform of black gowns and large headdresses with a white skull-and-bones emblem in front. Their activity was not limited to trying to kill blacks. They wanted to do away also with Catholics, Jews, Communists, union organizers, welfare workers, "and all isms which our forefathers came to this country to avoid." In pursuit of these aims, the Black Legion developed adventurous schemes to eliminate these enemies *en masse:* injecting typhoid germs into milk and cheese destined to be sold to undesirable neighborhoods and projecting cyanide gas into synagogues. One authority, Thomas L. Jones, writes, "Running through the literature and rhetoric of the Black Legion was the fear of an international Communist takeover of the United States. Black Legionnaires were ordered by their superiors to be prepared to take over Federal Government buildings with arms." The legion was finally broken in the 1930s, when it killed a Works Projects Administration organizer, one Charles Poole. The malefactors were rounded up and tried, and eleven received life sentences. Thirty more earned long prison terms as accessories.

The Klan watched these events with some dismay, and it has never recovered. Occasions for showing off its uniforms are increasingly rare, and almost certainly attended also by undercover agents spoiling for a dramatic case.

Uniforms of the Sporting Life

It seems not generally known that a vast crowd of baseball uniform hobbyists is constantly at work collecting, describing, arguing, and caring deeply about the subject. For example, here's an enthusiast going on in the customary fanatical style:

> On the subject of caps, Boston did go to the white-outlined B in 1946, but there was another change in the midfifties. They went from a large pointy sewn-on patch B to a smaller and neater-looking embroidered emblem, identical to the one used today. As near as I can tell, this change took place in 1955. . . . The 1975 Red Sox drawing shows a half-and-half navy/red cap crown. . . . This rare cap didn't last very long, and is seldom seen in souvenir shops. A friend of mine who is a lifelong fanatic was actually wearing one recently. I asked him what year it was from and he said 1974. I'm inclined to believe him. I can't recall if they changed caps during the 1975 regular season (from all blue or from half-and-half), but I am sure that during the post-season of 1975 the BoSox wore the all-red crown with a blue B and blue bill, as thousands of photographs will testify.

Another enthusiast, Jerry P. Cohen, decided to profit from this obsession by meticulously reproducing antique uniforms and selling them through his company, Ebbets Field Flannels.

His reproductions cover not just major leagues, but minor leagues and Negro and Latin leagues. Cohen said, "Baseball uniforms of the past had simple elegance. They were made of natural fabrics (primarily wool), and the colors were the result of tradition, practicality, and serendipity." The current style of baseball uniforms, emphasizing skin-tight fit and desperate attempts at slick masculinity, fills him with disdain. "One has only to look at the designs of the two newest major-league expansion teams to conclude that it might be safer in the late 1990s to listen to games on the radio."

At the beginning, baseball teams dressed much like cricketers, with white flannel trousers, white shirts, and little-boy caps. The Cincinnati team was apparently the first to play in what would be recognized today as "baseball uniforms" — baggy collarless short-sleeved shirts, often with long-sleeved undershirts beneath, and leather-belted oversize knickers worn with tall colored stockings. (Stirrup stockings came later.) The Red Sox, started in 1869, were known as the Cincinnati Red Stockings. Pin stripes were first worn in 1907 by the Chicago Cubs.

The current uniform rules laid down by major league baseball are nothing if not specific: "All players on a team shall wear uniforms identical in color, trim, and style, and all players' uniforms shall include minimal six-inch numbers on their backs. Any part of an undershirt exposed to view shall be of a uniform solid color for all players on a team. . . . No player whose uniform does not conform to that of his teammates shall be permitted to participate in a game." Some rules have to do with safety: "Glass buttons and polished metal shall not be used on a uniform. . . . No player shall attach anything to the heel or toe of his shoe other than the ordinary shoe plate or toe plate. Shoes with pointed spikes similar to golf or track shoes shall not be worn." If either league decides to allow players' names to appear on their uniforms, they must be last names only, and cute names or nicknames (like Dizzy Dean) are expressly forbidden.

Why do managers, commonly superannuated and often embarrassingly obese, always appear uniformed in the dugout or on the field? Answer: because when the game was new, the manager was one of the players. (Connie Mack was one of the few who refused to dress like his team, the Philadelphia Athletics. He stuck with a business suit.)

Baseball, of all the popular sports, is an old, highly traditional game, and it has never been comfortable with the blatant commercialism apparent in, say, motor racing or football. The National Football League, for example, goes so far as to employ retired players as "police" to make sure that corporate sponsors are getting their money's worth, that the Gatorade tubs are clearly marked and highly visible. If a football player wants to wear gloves made by a company that hasn't paid up, he must use tape to cover that company's logo.

The indefatigable efforts of commerce to demean the game can be inferred from the labors required of Ralph Nader. His organization, Commercial Alert, in Washington, recently sent a fervent letter to Allan H. Selig, commissioner of baseball:

> Dear Mr. Selig:
>
> We strongly urge Major League Baseball to reject any proposal to place advertisements on baseball uniforms. . . . You can honor the memories and the shared traditions of baseball, and the great players who have worn baseball uniforms, by refusing to sell the space on baseball uniforms to corporate advertisers. . . . Please don't emulate NASCAR, whose drivers already look like walking commercial billboards. . . . Don't destroy the dignity of baseball. . . . Will you defend baseball, or will you sell it out to big-buck advertisers?

Soon it may be necessary to write to the Army and Navy and Marines and Air Force, urging them not to proceed with their plans to sew great colored patches on their uniforms advertising Budweiser and Trojans.

THOSE WHO HAVE followed basketball over the years have doubtless wondered at some curious changes in the players'

uniforms. When the sport began to generate national interest, the uniform was much like the track-and-field outfit: lightweight sleeveless tank top and short shorts. The assumption must have been that if a uniform was fit for hurdlers, it would also do for basketball. But in the 1990s a remarkable change occurred: the shorts started to enlarge into loose-fitting baggy pants extending down almost to the knees. Some say the style became the vogue in 1991, when Michael Jordan, who chose to dress this way, won his first championship. Despite their ugly appearance (which has been imitated in men's swimming trunks), baggy shorts are in no way restricting and are actually easier to play in. Some players even favor extra large shorts, loose at the waist and immensely long in the legs, which in action tend to slip down, adding to the notably unathletic air of sloppiness. (The parallel change in men's swimsuits invites questions like, Is the cause a kind of neo-puritanism, an urge to drape, and thus disguise, the sexual parts of the body? The desire of swimmers to resemble basketball players? An impulse to pretend that swimming and nonswimming are somehow the same thing?)

It is when one turns to football uniforms that one sees something rare in athletic wear, a significant and ultimately melodramatic relation between form and function. The shoulder boards of the Russian army and the United States Navy are not there to protect the shoulder. A different scene altogether is projected in American football, both professional and collegiate. No one wants his collarbone broken repeatedly, and the protective and aesthetic functions — need one add *sexual?* — of the shoulder pads merge.

The game was made up by college boys, which speaks volumes about certain of its techniques and traditions. The first informal intercollegiate contest, between Rutgers and Princeton, took place in 1869, and the players had no protective equipment at all. They dressed in the sweaters and knickers they wore in the classroom. No one wore anything like a helmet or shoulder padding, and the game was not yet a sport for heavyweights. When the University of Alabama took up the game in 1892, the average weight of its players was 148 pounds. No one knew yet that the game was going to become an indispensable American contribution to the history of human violence, in the tradition of boxing and (fake) wrestling. Nor could one have predicted that the game would marry television until at, say, the Super Bowl, approximately half the time would be related to football, the other half to the huckstering of cars, beer, and similar presumably masculine necessities. As football's delicious violence increased, the uniform changed to an almost wholly protective outfit, a sort of post-medieval armor. In the old days, when you saw a fellow on the street with damaged ears and nose, you could infer that he was either a prizefighter or a football player. No more, what with the modern helmet and, most important, its face mask. Now, when a professional player retires, he may look elderly but he no longer looks beaten up.

In the *Journal of American Culture,* Professor Charlotte A. Jirousek, of Cornell, examined the close relation between the properly uniformed football player, with his padded shoulders and thighs, and the exaggerated ideal of male musculature dominating the body-building culture. (It would be rude and perhaps irrelevant at this point to refer to Hitler's apparent idea that shoulders are the prime index of male perfection, but if there's no political relation, there is certainly a cultural one.) "The power of this image," wrote Jirousek, "has contributed to a national obsession with physical fitness and sport." And she noted, "The most dramatic changes in the ideal [male] silhouette occurred after the introduction of regularly televised football in the 1960s." Looking back several decades, one can see that, "like football stars, movie stars seemed to become more broad shouldered as time passed." Jirousek's conclusion? "The upper body as envisaged in the image of the uniformed football hero has provided an unrealistic standard of male strength and beauty."

A memorable example of the way any well-known uniform, athletic, military, or even postal, tends to present to the populace, no matter how resistant or skeptical, a standard of virtue, beauty, efficiency, or power.

TO GET AN immense outdoor audience of strangers to chant silly words in unison certainly requires efficiency and power, usually attended by beauty — if not always by virtue. But the term "cheerleaders" conveys two quite different impressions. One is of the classic collegiate boy and girl on the football sidelines, he in school sweater and white duck or flannel trousers, she with white skirt and ankle socks. Both wear sneakers. He wields a large megaphone; she, one or more colored pompoms. Their expressions are sincere and optimistic.

The other image is distinctly sexy, popularized by professional football teams like the Dallas Cowboys and the Miami Dolphins. Here one finds uniformed groups with the chorines' look of unwavering smiles and minimal dress. One classic uniform features navel display above tight hot pants, along with white boots and a white bra attached to strip-show sleeves.

Regardless of the different appeal of the two types of cheerleaders, uniformity is indispensable. Even the staid flash-card performers at old-time football games had to wear uniforms of white shirts and bow ties, and sometimes bellboy-style caps. The young women constituting the other type must look like "mating organisms," as one observer pointed out. They must all enact the part of the "unattainable male macho dream girl," and there can be no deviation from that soft-porn look.

But it is strictly theatrical. Most cheerleaders for professional teams are really, as Mary Ellen Hanson, a professor of American studies, explains in *Go! Fight! Win!: Cheerleading in American Culture,* subject to "a degree of regimentation which goes beyond military discipline." They must follow strict rules of behavior designed to keep them objects merely of fantasy, never of sexual availability. No matter that they feature tits and ass, cleavage and high thighs, the come-on looks are only for chill sideline display. And, like chorus girls, they must look essentially alike. To be heeded by them, as well as by the more innocent-looking high school cheerleaders, is the injunction "Your uniforms should be exactly like those of the other cheerleaders. Don't vary as much as a collar button."

Useful to both collegiate and professional cheerleaders is Cheer Athletics, a Dallas training school focusing on such gymnastics as precision back flips and other elements of the art of tumbling. One favorite trick is to have the girl, upward extended arm, standing on one foot in the elevated hand of a boy. In addition to trainers, the teaching staff includes choreographers for the more elaborate routines. The more one knows about the arcana of cheerleading, the more it seems a sport in itself, for at its best it is highly athletic and dangerous. It is really an original uniformed sport, unknown before the twentieth century except on burlesque show stages and in circuses.

It is probably true that questions of class do not really attach to athletic outfits, although one may remember that the former obligatory whites of tennis once had the power to imply that the wearer was not a guttersnipe. One survival of the all-white motif is the uniform of serious enthusiasts of fencing. They require a protective mask, once made of mesh, but now, increasingly, of Plexiglas, with a padded bib to protect the neck from wayward assaults of the opponent's foil. Worn beneath the white top is a plastron, an underarm protector of the foil-flourishing arm and that side of the torso. Most familiar is the white form-fitting jacket, with the strap between the legs to keep it in position. Below the jacket, white knickers, high tube socks, and white fencing shoes — like light track shoes but without the spikes. In America there are only two exceptions to the all-white apparel: honorific patches may be sewn onto the nonmoving arm, and fencers may write their name, but only in blue ink, on their uniformed backs or legs. The only major change in this uniform over the decades has been a nod to technology, the addition of a light metallic lamé, which, when a hit has occurred, closes a circuit and signals an undeniable *touché*.

Next to the whites worn by a chef, the fencer's uniform is probably the most archaic and traditional in current use, deriving from the age when swordsmanship was an indispensable civil and military skill. Like the chef's double-breasted jacket, with its high collar, turn-back cuffs, and cloth buttons, the fencer's uniform suggests an aristocratic past many are unwilling to forget entirely. One recalls how recently that age vanished. In George Patton's early days in the Army, one of his triumphs was inventing an efficient new shape for the cavalry saber, suggesting that its use was not yet out of the question.

Stigmatic Uniforms

Uniforms divide into two rough categories: honorific and stigmatic. Honorific: the attire of police, McDonald's fast-food servers, United States Marines, the clergy. Stigmatic: the orange coveralls worn by prisoners, widely familiarized by the dress of Timothy McVeigh as depicted in a TV clip repeatedly shown after his arrest. Some county sheriffs have put their prisoners back into the old-fashioned broad stripes, and added the distinction of colors to distinguish types of malefactors: minimum security convicts wear green on white stripes; medium security, black on white (as in old films about prison life); and red on white for maximum security. It is beginning to be understood that striped prison wear is superior to solid orange because of the risk that escapees may resemble highway workers or sanitation employees. Either way, it is the sheriff who benefits politically when television shows a newly imprisoned law breaker. As Thomas Vinciguerra, a journalist, explained, "One sheriff, Gerald Hege of Davidson County, N.C., notes that in 1994 he won election by 227 votes. Then he clad his inmates in stripes. At his next election, he won by 5,000 votes. 'The public loves them,' he said of the stripes."

Both the striped and the plain color uniforms have neither pockets nor trouser cuffs, where prisoners might conceal weapons or drugs. Despite objections from the ACLU, etc., the state of Michigan has disallowed normal clothes as wear for inmates, requiring them to wear dark blue (the naval influence again?) two-piece cotton uniforms with a single large orange stripe running down each leg and arm. There are over 130,000 prisoners in Michigan, and there were budget objections to supplying each with two sets of the new uniform, together with three T-shirts, nine sets of underwear, two sets of thermal underwear, and one winter coat — all specially made without seams, pockets, or cuffs.

The upshot was inevitable. "Convicts at an Oregon state prison have sold their own line of designer prison clothes since 1990." Who buys? asks the *Detroit News*. "What free person would want to look like an inmate? Young people. 'If it will upset us, they'll wear it,' says Robert Butterworth, a psychologist who focuses on adolescents. The current style of baggy, ill-fitting clothes started in prison. The reason: belts are taken away from inmates so they're not used as a weapon or to commit suicide. So low-riding pants are a prison tradition."

During World War II, German and Italian prisoners held by the Americans wore used U.S. Army fatigues with the letters PW enlarged in white on the back of the jacket. The seams and pockets were left intact, attempts at escape being very rare, because most of the prisoners were pleased to be alive and well and nicely fed for a change, or were discouraged from escape by the emphatic isolation of their camps.

The situation was distinctly different for many civilians in Germany and countries controlled by the Reich. For one thing, Jews could be identified by their worn-out clothes, for they were forbidden to enter any store selling new clothing. This sorry situation dated from September 19, 1941, when the Nazis decided that all Jews over the age of six living in German-controlled territory would have to give notice of their loathsome proximity by wearing on their outer clothing a five-inch-wide yellow cloth Star of David bearing the word *Jude* in black pseudo-Hebrew letters. This was bad enough. But worse, and very Nazi, was the ruling that Jews would have to pay for these stars, as if they were honorific. Jews had to fork over ten pfennigs for each star. The Jews called it the David Star; the Nazis, the Jewish Star. It was like a badge, and a badge of shame it was designed to be. If it was a badge, can it be classified as a uniform? Professor Peter Gay, formerly of Yale, who was there as a child, senses that the star constituted a uniform. "Jews," he recalls, "were to be identified by a special uniform." It was a uniform because it identified a visible group of people and set them off from others.

Before this time, Jewish property had been seized, and Jews were forbidden to practice professions, sit on benches in parks, or buy what they might need; a common shop sign read, "Foods in Short Supply Are Not Sold to Jews." Since by this time it was virtually impossible for Jews to flee, the object now was to humiliate them and make them feel "ashamed," as if they'd done something wrong. As Marion Kaplan wrote in *Between Dignity and Despair: Jewish Life in Nazi Germany,*

> The introduction of the star signaled a new stage in persecution. "This was the most difficult day in the twelve years of hell," according to Victor Klemperer. Every person wearing a star "carried his ghetto with him, like a snail its house." With the yellow star blazing from their coats Jews could be identified, vilified, and attacked with impunity. Those who had earlier dared to circumvent shopping rules, limitations on public transport, or restrictions on entertainment could no longer do so unless they removed their star. This was a severe crime; even a loose star could be cause for sending its wearer to a concentration camp.

One German army Einsatzgruppe, scouring the roads of rural Russia for Jews, reported, "During the check along the roads, 135 people, mostly Jews, were apprehended. The Jews were not wearing the Jewish badge. . . . 127 people were shot." They were out of uniform.

And in a concentration camp, what uniform was an incarcerated Jew obliged to wear? One similar to that worn by the other prisoners, as if he had done something terribly wrong. Donald Watt, a British soldier captured early in the war and confined to Auschwitz, where he survived by helping to stoke the fires beneath the cremation furnaces, described the Auschwitz uniform: trousers and jacket of pseudo-linen artificial material, with vertical faded blue stripes. Primo Levi remembered the long striped overcoats worn by some lucky long-term prisoners, inexplicably not yet gassed to death.

Sewn onto the common uniform were cloth badges, each identifying the crime that had landed the wearer in the camp: green triangle with numbers, a civil criminal; red triangle, a political criminal; pink triangle, a homosexual; red triangle with yellow star, a Jew. The SS guards especially despised the so-called asocials, who had escaped once from a prison camp or had distinguished themselves as public loafers, unwilling to work for the nation. Their uniforms bore a black triangle, and the SS guards, unwilling to overlook the presumed insult to their black uniform, plied their whips, truncheons, rifle butts, and gallows with special enthusiasm.

The "uniform" was the same in summer and winter, in heat and terrible cold, and lice always went with it. To add to the shame and the punishment, the prisoners were given no underclothes. Donald Watt spoke of "scrounging an extra shirt which I turned into a pair of underpants by tying the sleeves around my waist."

As we have seen, the Germans had a thing about buttons. The rules for prisoners at Auschwitz prescribed that precisely five buttons must appear on the front of the jacket. Prisoners were forbidden to leave their huts with the jackets unbuttoned, and at the same time there was no way to sew buttons on, the possession of needle and thread being forbidden. A perfect Catch-22. But at many of the extermination camps in Poland, the matter of uniforms was moot. Prisoners had no time to don them, being stripped naked and escorted to the gas chamber immediately upon arrival.

Not everyone was debased by uniform. Some specially privileged prisoners wore more civilized garb. For example, the women's orchestra at Auschwitz, which supplied rhythm and melody for the work-commandos as they marched out in the morning and marched back in the evening. The female musicians wore navy blue skirts and white blouses, presumably out of respect for the Germanic instrumental repertory — except, of course, works by the Jew Felix Mendelssohn.

Weirdos

Sometimes it seems that everyone likes to imagine being a part of the military. Recently, at a men's fashion show in Milan, it became clear that the designers counted on selling heaps of garments closely imitating military wear: pseudo trench coats, epaulets in gold, Eisenhower jackets in costly fabrics, and the like. It must be great fun to imagine yourself a soldier without risk of physical, mental, or moral damage. This sort of military romanticism you'd think the Vietnam War had put a final stop to, but no. It flourishes, and one place where it flourishes most vividly is among "re-enactors," as they like to call themselves. These people, having missed World War II, Korea, and Vietnam, never tasted the thrill of being machine-gunned and mortared and thus escaped, unlike former ground troops, lifelong bodily and spiritual damage. Not having endured real military experience, they get excited by faking it, wearing authentic uniforms of the appropriate periods and indulging fantasies of heroism, largely on weekends. Playing soldiers used to be appropriate only among small boys. Now it is widespread among grown-ups, who dress like troops in order to re-enact the bloodiest of infantry slaughters. Missing are the screams of the wounded and the vomiting and crying of those close to them. It is puzzling to know what to call these odd neighbors of ours. Some onlookers may prefer the term "weirdos." Others, peering more deeply into psychiatric causes, may go further and call these folks "sickos."

One intelligent inquirer into the sick dimension of this curious uniformitis is Valerie Steele, of New York's Fashion Institute of Technology. Her book *Fetish: Fashion, Sex, and Power* (1996) nicely illuminates the pathology of this behavior. "Military uniforms," she writes, "are probably the most popular prototype of the fetishest uniform because they signify hierarchy (some command, others obey) as well as membership in . . . an all-male group whose function involves the legitimate use of physical violence. Soldiers can shoot and stab without constraint." Fake uniforms confer the illusion of power upon those who have none, she emphasizes in her chapter "The Cult of the Uniform." Intimately connected with the fantasy workings of the sadomasochistic imagination are uniforms associated with official cruelty, like those of the German SS, imitations of which you can buy on the Internet from Waffen.SS.com. One company selling Third Reich Reproductions is careful in the descriptions of its wares to reflect accurately the idiom and understanding of those who proudly wore the original outfits, that is, "National Socialist soldiers in the struggle against Bolshevism." (So *that's* what the war was really about.) Equipped with the right uniform and accessories, you can join the "1st SS Re-enactors of California." Another dealer in SS uniforms and supplies enjoins the public to "find out why 70 million people did [support Nazism, we are invited to finish the sentence]," assisted by a full-face photo of Der Führer. As a friend of mine is fond of saying, "The Nazi beast sleeps between wars."

Because military uniforms, as we have seen, emphasize the sexual authority of their wearers by fitting tightly and calling attention to the shoulders, wearing simulacra of them seems to bolster the selfhood of the feeble in body as well as mind. An ad in an obviously sadomasochistic magazine appears to give the whole show away, offering both rubber wear and uniforms. Here, an enthusiast of pornographic reading may obtain such titles as *Our Boys in Uniforms, Sluts in Uniform,* the ubiquitous *Naughty Nurses,* and, for the gay, *Soldiers of Sodom* and *Leather Boot Camp.*

So widespread is the current culture of would-be power-wielding troop impersonators that highly successful businesses have arisen to supply them with the necessary gear. One such company, which calls itself U.S. Cavalry, issues a handsome catalog of uniforms and equipment. It is careful to designate its outlets by emphasizing their proximity to such army centers as Fort Bragg and Fort Benning. By personally calling at one of these stores, you will experience the feeling of being drafted into the ground forces and getting equipped for the greatest outdoor adventure of your life — infantry combat. From this company and others like it you can order genuine Purple Heart and Bronze Star medals to assist your fantasized new identity. Battle-dress uniform is available, even in kiddies' sizes (2–18), together with helmets, body armor, and dog tags with your own name on them. You can buy silencers for firearms so that you won't alert the enemy as you crawl toward him, prepared to knife him to death silently. Special Forces berets are, of course, to be had, and so are air rifles resembling M-16s as well as pistols hard to distinguish from real military Colt .45s. And weirdos aspiring to impress onlookers can avail themselves of olive-drab T-shirts identifying the wearer as belonging to the POLICE or an official unit performing works of RESCUE.

If you are a re-enactor more adventurous than the ordinary Civil War type, you can choose which World War II German or Italian unit you want to be "in." For example, you can "join" the 81st Reggimento Fanteria. "This unit," states Bill Bethke, its organizer, "is dedicated to the accurate re-creation of the World War II infantry combat soldier serving in the Italian army between the years 1940 to 1943." If you don't like imagining defeat and ignominious surrender, you may want to serve in a Panzergrenadier unit on the Eastern Front during the last two years of the war. Such a unit, we are promised, aims at being "as period as possible," and thus it may supply the weirdo imagination with the experience of slaughtering any Jews and commissars left alive by the SS working out in front.

Sometimes the re-enactors in SS uniforms go too far, incurring the risk of being banned from the use of open lands for their performances. The re-enactor Larry Mayo, an authority on World War II groups, recognizes that some attract their share of "psychopathic loners" and "borderline screwballs," and he advises the others to ferret them out, lest the fun be spoiled for the clean and sincere. He writes, "There is an incredible amount of stupidity exhibited by many WW II re-enactors." Like those who go around in public wearing Nazi uniforms and loading cars bound for a re-enactment site with weapons, fireworks, and other re-enactment impedimenta. As Mayo reports:

> One of our unit members was recently stopped on the way to an event on a traffic violation. He was in a hurry, and had his uniform on. The cop saw the uniform, rousted him, searched his car, and jailed him on a weapons violation. The uniform was all it took. There are a lot of idiots who don't seem to realize that WW II is the only major type of re-enactment where those who fought and suffered in it are still alive, along with the animosity and ill feelings it generated between peoples. To this type of re-enactor, the war is a personal fantasy. . . . Sad and scary.

Mayo notes that one group of re-enactors was forbidden access to the U.S. 1st Division Museum in Illinois when its SS flag appeared in a news photo. As he says, "We face the potential loss of all federal and public lands and an open accusation of being a front for terrorist training if we lack the ability to supervise the hobby."

The public appearance of some of these weirdos can be profoundly embarrassing. On the site of the D-day landings on Utah Beach in Normandy, as the London *Guardian* reported recently, there was seen, in the "overpriced Café Roosevelt," a "thirty-something man in D-day vintage combat gear, sporting an authentic entrenching tool strapped to his webbing belt." A memorably sick man.

Less openly psychiatric are the numerous groups of Civil

War re-enactors whose rosters have swollen to include British as well as American fantasists. Their needs are supplied by Sutlers, an elegant uniform company in Britain specializing in both Union and Confederate garb, but it will also make to order uniforms from the two World Wars. Knowing the energy and persistence of the re-enactors of all types, one should not be surprised to find that passionate uniform fetishists have spread out from the United States to be found worldwide, and now, in both Britain and America, Civil War battle re-enactment is a serious business, with frantic attention to authenticity. (One senses that many re-enactors, in addition to being frustrated combat soldiers, are also frustrated actors.) "When it comes to buying a hat," declares the Sutlers catalog, "the majority of American Civil War re-enactors usually take their time searching for '*the hat*' that they feel comfortable in. In fact, when the right hat has been purchased it often becomes a part of that person and stays with them rather like a trademark, for the rest of their re-enacting life."

Sutlers can provide, for both sides, authentic-looking buttons, belt buckles, and insignia, gold- or silver-plated and embroidered. The buyer can arrive at the ersatz battlefield wearing shoulder bars of any officer's rank, from second lieutenant to lieutenant general. Those choosing more modestly to impersonate noncommissioned officers can acquire corporals', sergeants', and sergeant majors' cloth chevrons. The weirdos' quest for absolute authenticity may lead them finally to Sutlers' wooden-handled period shaving brush or its wooden-handled period toothbrush.

The Sutlers catalog also contains information about the "Southern Skirmish Association. A Living History and Re-enactment Society," based in Wiltshire, England. "We are currently recruiting for the Union Army," the society has announced, adding an appeal to the lonely, bored, adolescent, and somewhat sick: "Do your weekends lack glamour and excitement? If the answer is yes, then our Society can be for you." The SSA offers "undiluted escapism" and is proud to be, like many such organizations in the United Kingdom, a member of NARS, the National Association of Re-Enactment Societies. A recruit-ment come-on is an attractive photo of one of the associa-tion's encampments in 1997, depicting period tents lined up and Union soldiers milling about, doubtless showing one an-other how authentic their uniforms are.

But Sutlers does not propose to stop with the American Civil War, full of gratifying imaginary gore and horror as it may be. It promises to branch out soon and offer uniforms of Napoleonic, Zulu, and Boer wars as well as the American Indian wars. And for any re-enactors lusting after military glory, Sutlers can sup-ply a phony Victoria Cross.

Comprehensive as the re-enactors' ambitions to achieve ab-solute authenticity are, they neglect certain details, like the writhing of the wounded, their attempts to thrust back into their abdomens their protruding intestines, and their weeping and calling on Mother. But bullet, bayonet, and shell-fragment damage can perhaps be simulated with ketchup, carefully de-ployed. And for greater authenticity, you could buy a quart of blood from your nearest slaughterhouse.

Ernest Hemingway, Semi-Weirdo

It would be unfair to designate Hemingway, because of his delight in playing soldier, a weirdo, but it would not be unfair to call him a semi-weirdo. Never a genuine army officer, or even a soldier, he had seen some war, first, as a member of a World War I Ambulance Corps, then as a war correspondent attending the Spanish Civil War, and finally a correspondent in Europe during World War II. He knew enough about infantry fighting to describe it, faultlessly and brilliantly, in *A Farewell to Arms* and in many short stories, but he was always a noncombatant, a role he felt, in his boyism, no temptation to advertise.

In the First World War, he served in Northern Italy as a Red Cross ambulance driver, a member of the American Volunteer Ambulance Service. Among his duties was bicycling up to the front line and distributing chocolate, cigarettes, and similar comforts to the Italian troops facing the Austrians. Because he bore the assimilated rank of lieutenant, the uniform he wore was a U.S. Army officer's, with classy leather puttees. He was never part of the Italian army, although after the war, back among his stateside audience in Oak Park, Illinois, he liked to sport an "Italian cape." When he could, he wore an Italian officer's uniform with, instead of the normal U.S. high collars, more gentlemanly lapels and necktie. His being badly wounded on one of his trips to the front gave him a chance to play the hero, which he did for the rest of his life. Sometimes he lied about his actual experience in Red Cross uniform, which might seem embarrassingly close to the work of the Doughnut Dollies who furnished cocoa and cookies to American soldiers in subsequent wars. He was caught out once in a lie by his biographer Carlos Baker, and the phrase "fought with the Italian army" was changed to "served with."

When the Spanish Civil War came along in the 1930s, he reported from Madrid as a correspondent for the North American Newspaper Alliance. Some think he departed from the truth in suggesting the dangers he faced, for he seldom failed to mention his bravery — which was never in doubt — and his skill in military affairs. As another Hemingway biographer, Kenneth S. Lynn, observed, "It was the first but not the last instance in which he would publicly hint that he knew so much about warfare that the Loyalist commanders viewed him as a consultant." Lynn went on to term this terrible need of Hemingway to effuse unearned authority his "military Munchausenism."

In the Second World War, where, like all the war correspondents, he held the assimilated rank of captain for purposes of lodging and rations, he liked to pretend to be a real infantry captain, although as a correspondent he was forbidden to carry arms and certainly to lead troops. He again wore an officer's uniform, with little gold U.S. pins on both sides of his shirt collar and jacket lapels, and, on the left shoulder, where a noble divisional patch would be, he had to wear the nonbellicose and therefore humiliating patch reading War Correspondent.

The proper uniform proved insufficient to feed his fantasies of being an infantry officer, and a better one than the real ones he saw as he moved about, so in France he removed his correspondent's insignia and collected a group of un-uniformed partisans, heavily armed. These he "commanded." He got away with this until, near Rambouillet, in 1944, he was charged with misbehavior and had to lie his way out — and to see to it that his friends did the same.

This being the third war he had attended as a noncombatant, his impulse to pose as an expert on infantry tactics and a man chosen to command seemed to grow. With his wife Mary Welsh he tended to act as if he were a platoon leader and she a mere soldier, and not a very bright or responsible one at that. She once said to him, "I will not submit for the rest of my life to being ordered about."

Everyone noticed that with those who were weaker, he took the part of head cheese. Notably, in all his writing he shunned the role of an enlisted man, and whether imagining himself fighting in Italy or Spain or France, fantasized about being in charge — and being successful and admired as the one in command. Writing to his wife in the fall of 1944, he assured her of his love by some exhibitionistic military cant that he assumed would impress her: "I am as committed as an armored column in a narrow defile where no vehicle can turn and without parallel roads." His lies about imagined military service — in China, at sea, in the air, in the Second World War with the 22nd Infantry — he delivered with total commitment. He had been shot through the scrotum, he indicated, and not just once but twice. Martha Gellhorn, one of his wives and an experienced war correspondent, said, prophetically, "He will end in the nut house."

One result of all this was his appallingly bad novel *Across the River and Into the Trees* (1950), where he projected himself into the admirable character Colonel Richard Cantwell, giving him opinions that Hemingway would have liked to hold if he'd been in the colonel's place as a regimental commander and onetime brigadier general. He took all this very seriously. The sense of irony he'd possessed in his early career seemed, in his later years, to leave him, as if his lifelong ambition had been to resemble a simplified comic strip hero without subtlety, remorse, or the power of self-criticism.

He feared being taken for a coward, and his military fantasizing was a way of defending himself from imputations that were, on the face of it, implausible. His happy illegal participation in two RAF bomber flights through the flak is ample evidence of his courage. His lies were not necessary. They were psychopathic and, to his audiences, intolerable.

In November 1944, Second Lieutenant Jack Crawford, a

field-commissioned, three-times wounded survivor of the Battle of Hürtgen Forest, came upon Hemingway and his idol Colonel Lapham drinking in a bar in Spa, Belgium. Lapham asked the lieutenant to join them, and Crawford reported:

> As we drank and talked I felt he was full of it and this really wasn't his war. He was telling tales of hijinks in Paris. I finally got pissed off and said he should come up to my battalion with me in the Hürtgen to see what the war was really like instead of sitting back thirty miles from the front line. The Colonel jumped on me and said I was out of line, so I stood up, saluted the Colonel, and said, "Fuck you, Hemingway," and walked out.

Hemingway's whole sorry career of personal military imagining can be imputed in part to his living in times when military uniforms were everywhere and were held to signify a desirable kind of manliness. He wanted to be a uniformed hero, and he might have been an admirable one. But unfortunately, he was only a writer, and that caused all the trouble.

Uniformity in American
Higher Learning

Recently a spokesman for a college fraternity accused of regrettable physical mistreatment of its new members declared, in defense of that tradition, "It is necessary to iron out the flaws that a person might have." For "flaws," a student of uniformities, both the compulsory and the freely elected, may want to substitute an idea like "signs of integrity" or "intellectual talent" or "taste" or "individuality." These will be ironed out ultimately, when the boy becomes a real-estate or automobile salesman or a corporate executive, but we should notice how early the ironing-out process is likely to begin, and, more striking, how many, in their loneliness and uncertainty, reach out for it.

The sixty national fraternities are attached to over six hundred American and Canadian universities, but they are notably absent from aged institutions like Harvard and Princeton. The reason is that such institutions were founded well before the educational Westward Movement, encouraged by the Land Grant Act of 1862. This helped establish "state universities" and agricultural and mechanical institutes in the new West. The old Eastern universities already had their own exclusive boys' clubs (Porcellian, Skull and Bones), often accused, then and now, of excessive snobbery.

A new lust for reputations of probity and civic responsibility has followed the national disgust at the sadistic paddling, tormenting, and compulsory overdrinking that appear to be the fraternities' main business. Deaths from sudden alcoholic brain damage are now harder to conceal than they used to be. But fraternity members still seem to resist the natural process of growing up, causing one critic to label their groups "Addictive Organizations." And the power of the current business-school ethic and style can be inferred from a defense of fraternities — sororities, too — by one loyal member: "Fraternities and sororities are not all bad. They are excellent networking groups for later life." Universities in Europe also generate their uniformity mechanisms (German drinking groups, French arguing groups), but the group consciousness seldom survives into later life. "Reunions" are almost wholly a New World invention, and one pursuing the topic must wonder whether this American groupism isn't a result of a specifically American loneliness. Here, social identity, unlike the tradition still alive in Europe, tends not to be generically received. One must construct it for oneself, and it's a distinct assistance to adhere to a collection of similars to avoid nonentity. The United States is a nonhistorical environment, and individual identity must be earned.

But the young American male need not hunker down in a group like a fraternity to risk anxiety over being caught out of uniform. And the same goes for the female of the species, who is perhaps allowed a bit more invention in her get-up. Fraternity boys engage in all sort of levities and pranks, but not a single "brother" would think of appearing in, say, colorful tights. The brothers in their millions are clad in the obligatory uniform of their decade. It used to comprise, at least in the East, khakis or gray flannel trousers, button-down shirts, tweed jackets, and loafers. Crew neck sweaters and corduroys were also acceptable. Professor Edward Said of Columbia recalls what everyone — *everyone* — looked like at his prep school and at Princeton, where he went next: "My classmates either were or tried to be cut from the same cloth . . . everyone wore the same clothes (white bucks, chinos, button-down shirts, and tweed jackets)." Getting the shirts right was particularly important, and in button-downs, light blue was virtually obligatory. Said testified that he once witnessed two Princetonians at work soliciting the desired worn-out look by applying sandpaper to the collars of new, and of course blue, shirts.

In England the conformity scene is even worse. There, in some public schools (that is, private schools), the students still wear black tailcoats with striped trousers, white shirts, with ties of required pattern, and straw boaters. One school, Queen Elizabeth's Hospital, in Bristol, kits the lads out in dark blue eighteenth-century jackets with lace neckware of the period and brass buttons. At lesser schools, boys are obliged to wear woolen shorts with high stockings, school blazers with the school badge on the left pocket, and caps with short visors, a style halfway between what used to be called a beanie and the headwear of the Sturm Abteilung. It is to Eton's credit that it finally abandoned the mock grown-up formal wear in the 1960s.

Changes in the general student uniform are probably faster in America, and now the once-sacred loafers have been largely replaced by "running shoes," reflecting the current power of the imagery of athleticism and "fitness." In the same way, the jacket or sweater has given way to the parka, as if daily life involved some sort of mountain hiking. For that purpose, the universal backpack suggests not books but adventurous contents, like pemmican or extra crampons. And, of course, jeans and denim jackets have enjoyed their moments of popularity, as have, in the Northwest, Pendleton wool jackets. But still, not one single male university student, no matter his courage elsewhere, has dared appear in colorful tights.

For at least the last half-century the college man has owned one suit (dark, for interviews), one sports jacket, khakis, jeans, and a couple of sweaters, and, before the hiking culture took over, a pair of penny loafers. This uniformity, this rigid avoidance of the whirligigs of "fashion," suggests that Americans between the ages of eighteen and twenty-one are especially terrified of putting a foot wrong and incurring ridicule or humiliation. They must play it safe, especially when they conceive of themselves in environments capable of determining their whole future, in which public "success" is the goal. They often speak in a way that seems to celebrate individuality, but they almost never venture to practice it. Too risky. Once they have grown up and been beaten about by life a bit, they may feel safer in practicing some singularity, even if loneliness results. But please, not yet.

Japan as a Uniform Culture

The motive of avoiding sartorial criticism at all costs at American universities dominates one whole culture abroad. That culture is Japan.

Even when finding fault with it, it is well to bear in mind the awful things it has been through: having its cities burned down, reacting to atomic bombing, losing the war humiliatingly, and being commanded for a generation not by a member of its own society but by a total stranger named MacArthur. It is forbidden to have its own army, although it's seen plenty of the armies of others, comprising lots of drunken GIs and marines on brief drinking and sex leaves from Vietnam. It operates under a constitution devised by strangers, and it is not at all certain about what, in government, is right or wrong. That is, what is permitted, for Nanny is always watching.

Asked what makes Japan tick, a long-time observer answered in one word: "insecurity." And explained, "This pervasive anxiety . . . helps to mobilize millions of people each day." Another observer, who teaches at a Japanese women's college, notes the universal conviction that one is being watched all the time. One's outsides and general appearance are thus all-important, and behavioral uniformity there provides a safer refuge from the stigma of singularity than it does in most places. The result is, as one bright visitor noticed, that "everyone above the rank of carpenter in Japan wears a uniform." Sometimes with a white Sam Browne belt, often with white gloves. One student, delighted to wear a school uniform like everyone else, declares, "We consider cooperation important, and being 'average' is highly regarded." (It pays sometimes to take a moment to imagine what the United States would be like if the Axis had won the Second World War: architecture everywhere like that of the Stony Brook campus of the State University of New York; government-issue utility clothing for all; compulsory group games.)

The womens' college teacher paid lots of attention to "the role of regulated dress" and to the whole world of Japanese uniformity. If signs of renewed real militarism are forbidden, uniforms and their usefulness in mass identification have flourished as an apparent compensation. Young hyperambitious businessmen wear the obligatory dark suit and white shirt, with harmless necktie. Taxi and bus drivers would prefer not to be seen without their white gloves. Security guards, tour guides, and elevator operators wear quasi-military uniforms. Young male schoolchildren uniformly wear yellow caps and carry oversized backpacks. Older male students wear navy blue uniforms, and older female students come on in strict navy-and-white ensembles, dark blue skirt (number of pleats rigorously specified) and white middy blouses with sailors' "flap" collars (the Japanese term for the appropriate female school garment is *sêra fuku,* sailor uniform). In some schools even the color of the shoelaces is specified and regulated. And the habit of uniformity goes on throughout adulthood. There are no casual Fridays in Japan, and virtually no casual anything.

Academic Full Dress

For male professors, daily academic uniform is either a suit (rare) or tweed jacket with gray flannel (sometimes corduroy) trousers. But for celebratory occasions, as in the military something more showy is customary; full academic regalia, seen at convocations and commencements, is the academy's equivalent of full dress.

During the nineteenth century, you wore ordinary clothes to a college commencement ceremony, although most of the faculty doubtless wore dark suits and dresses to honor the dignity of the occasion. But after 1895 things changed. A national conference on academic dress and ceremonies established the uniformities appropriate to the three academic degrees then granted: bachelor's, master's, and doctor's, with a different black gown for each. Here are the specifications, as laid down by the American Council of Education:

> The gowns used in American academic ceremonies vary according to the highest degree awarded to the wearer. The gown for the baccalaureate degree has pointed sleeves. It is designed to be worn closed. The gown for the master's degree has an oblong sleeve, open at the wrist. . . . The sleeve base hangs down in the traditional manner. . . . The rear part of its oblong shape is square cut, and the front has an arc cut away. Master's gowns may be worn

open or closed. The doctoral gown is more elaborate, faced down the front with black velvet and across the sleeves with three bars of the same; these facings and cross-bars may be of velvet of the color distinctive to the field of study to which the degree pertains. The doctoral gown has bell-shaped sleeves and may be worn open or closed.

The thing hanging down behind the wearer is a hood, most often exhibiting the colors of the institution granting the degree. An informal rule of thumb is, the longer the hood hangs down in the back, the grander the wearer. ("My hood is longer than your hood." How Virginia Woolf would have loved it.) In some universities and colleges, recipients of bachelor's degrees don't get any hood at all, either through their college's oversight or perhaps adherence to a policy that in the midst of hood-wearers, mere lowly bachelors should be stigmatized and thus encouraged to continue their achievements in the higher learning until they too can rise to the more honorable status of hood-wearers.

Academic full-dress headwear used to be simple. The black mortarboard (with gold tassel for Ph.D.s) was obligatory. But in the past fifty years or so, levities have crept in, and now one must choose whether to wear the standard mortarboard or a funny little four-cornered tam with a tassel on top. Some holders of doctor's degrees have been coming on in immensely wide pseudo-Renaissance caps of velvet — unwittingly funny, a satirist might emphasize, when worn by professors of marketing or accounting, not to mention soils. The popularity of these novel departures from traditional headgear has been simultaneous with the advent of colored, rather than black, doctoral gowns. Here, Harvard University must assume much of the blame, for it helped originate the modern movement in academic uniform. It granted its doctors of "philosophy" and other things the right to wear pinkish (in its view, crimson) gowns with contrasting black stripes on the sleeves. This departure from classic black opened the floodgates. Gaudy doctoral gowns appeared all over the country, and soon it became axiomatic that the worst universities were giving their least impressive doctors the flashiest gowns. (There's a principle here, perhaps implicitly Shakespearean.)

Colored gowns having appeared, further outrages were to come. On the two front velvet panels of the doctoral gown began to appear, on each side, little emblems, logos, and signifiers: university "arms" and seals and, worse, bragging emblems of various kinds. Doctors from Columbia (once King's College) have two matched crowns in front, Rutgers two little italic Q's (for Queen's), with founding date, 1766, beneath. The University of Michigan came up with two midget lamps of learning, Boston University its tasteless seal, etc. Makers of gowns for Protestant divines were not slow to perceive the possibilities, and some leaped to supply their velvet panels with copies of Albrecht Dürer's clichéd hands in praying position.

It may be remarked here that all this is a sad illustration, like the Navy's experience, of needless deviation from an eminently successful, well-known model, and it's especially sad in the world of learning, where (churches aside) history and tradition are most highly honored. The very implicit archaism of full-dress academic uniform is one of its meanings. The dressing-up of kindergarten kids in little caps and gowns is an abomination of taste displayed, alas, only in America.

It may be a comfort to realize that America is not the only place with curious academic uniforms. Britain until recently went even further. There, at least at an ancient university like Oxford, you had to put on a black gown for the slightest academic occasion, like a conference with your thesis adviser, not to mention your moral tutor. Without your gown, you'd not be allowed to write a final exam. And not just a gown. It had to be worn with *sub fusc,* a virtually untranslatable term meaning black suit or dress, black shoes, white shirt or blouse, and white piqué bow tie, which tends to grow dirtier with every wearing. And to have dinner in the dining hall, you also had to be thus gowned. The object of all this daily gownery was apparently to confer dignity on intellectual and related operations, which, if genuine, don't need it. Gowns like this also suggested exclusion of those not admitted to the mystery, and were thereby useful in elevating and maintaining the vain self-image of the adepts.

Pretties

There's a temptation to think of the uniform of the Swiss Guards at the Vatican as costumes, for they are pure Renaissance (fourteenth century, actually). These men engaged in protecting the pope wear jackets with bloused sleeves, bloused trousers, and stockings, all with gaudy vertical stripes of red, blue, and yellow, the colors of the Medici family's livery. There's a bit of white: the ruff around the neck and the gloves. The metal helmet, topped with a large red ostrich plume, resembles one that might have been worn by a soldier of Ponce de León.

The colorful uniforms identify a unit of some one hundred troops on daily guard duty. This is really a small army, and these are uniforms. Costume outfits resembling these are worn by the contestants in the annual frantic horse race, the *Palio,* in Siena, but are worn for only a day and lack uniformity.

Like the soldiers they are, the Swiss Guards live in a nearby barracks when not on duty at the various entrances to Vatican property. In the past, the unit was sometimes engaged in serious combat. In 1527, 147 Swiss Guards were killed when German and Spanish troops attacked the Papal States, and the current company-sized outfit is distinctly ready for battle. Since the attempt to assassinate the pope in 1981, Swiss Guards' training has included karate, judo, and expert use of assault weapons and shrewdly concealed firearms. They are even trained in using their ceremonial halberds (halberdiers, they are officially called) as stabbing and cutting weapons. And they know how to use for serious purposes the ceremonial sabers they often wear.

Contrary to tourist babble, neither Michelangelo nor Raphael designed the uniforms. Actually, they are very like Swiss army garb of the medieval period, and they are made by hand in the guards' own tailoring shop, together with their undress uniforms in dark blue, worn with berets.

The guards are recruited from German-speaking Swiss Catholic men who are aged nineteen to thirty and at least five feet nine inches tall. There are seven military ranks, from colonel on down, and only bachelors may be enlisted, although, with proper permission, they may marry during their service. When the pope travels, members of the guard travel with him, but in plainclothes, like U.S. Secret Service officers, and, like them, are armed and ready for action.

ALTHOUGH PERHAPS MORE pompous and melodramatic than pretty, the uniforms of the Roman Catholic Knights of Columbus should not be neglected. The organization was founded in 1882, but the uniformed branch, the Fourth Degree, dates only from 1902. It began in New York City, with a commitment to both patriotism and piety. Today, groups of these uniformed older men are likely to appear at Catholic ceremonies like funerals and wakes, and they often perform guard duty in formation when high-ranking prelates and other public figures must be overtly protected.

Soon after its founding, its official history says, "An up-to-date committee on uniform was appointed, and a neat uniform was adapted modeled on that of U.S. Navy officers, the appropriateness of the Naval uniform suggesting itself for a body that regards Columbus the Navigator and high Admiral as its patron." The official uniform ("full regalia") is suggestive not merely of naval officers, but of high officers with the rank of admiral, as the fore-and-aft hat with overflowing white adornment implies. The uniform requires the wearing of evening clothes, no matter the time of day, once white tie and tails, now black tie; a cape, whose different bright colors indicate rank or office; and a sword, depending from a baldric (a shoulder strap crossing the chest). White gloves complete the uniform. The sword, its straight hilt alluding to the fifteenth century, is silver for most members, gold for high officers like supreme and local masters.

The history of the organization is spattered with the usual struggles to achieve uniformity in dress. Christopher J. Kauffman, a historian of the order, noted that after the Second World War, newly awakened democratic impulses resulted in some unwelcome variations: Eisenhower jackets began appearing in Missouri, and some knights wore their military medals on their capes. To pacify these complainers, it was finally agreed that the "aristocratic" white tie and tails must go, the tuxedo remaining the official suit beneath the cape. But no adornment was allowed, not braid, medals, cords, or state and local badges. The only bits of insignia permitted are the badge of the order worn on the "chapeau" and the letters "K of C" on the stand-up collar of the cape. Together with the fancy Swiss Guards of the Vatican, the Knights of Columbus suggest a special Catholic enthusiasm for the idea of uniformed guards, prepared to ward off and dispatch lurking Protestant attacks. That is, the Reformation is still going on.

YOU'D HAVE TO be very old or very square — and aesthetically unashamed — to admit being thrilled once by pretty Nelson Eddy and Jeanette MacDonald singing Rudolf Friml's romantic ballads in the film *Rose Marie,* one of the hits of 1936. It cast Eddy, once a baritone star of the Philadelphia opera, as a member of the Royal Canadian Mounted Police, and Broadway soprano MacDonald as his sweetheart. Their unforgettable duets (all week I've been humming the one titled "Rose Marie")

were sentimental, romantic, and charming, implying a world with only happy endings for nice people, after the crooks were vanquished. Eddy's performance in *Rose Marie* did more than anything else to establish the bright red uniform of the RCMP as a Wholly Good Thing, an emblem of absolute moral cleanliness and noble behavior of all kinds.

The film aside, the RCMP uniform was extremely good-looking. Smoky Bear stiff-brimmed Stetson hat, red serge tunic with black standing collar and gauntlet cuffs, black Sam Browne belt, black breeches with bright yellow side stripes, and black laced boots and spurs. A gallant white lanyard was attached to the black-holstered pistol, the other end forming a loop around the neck. The whole get-up was so dashing and attractive, even when pictured in mere black and white, that I'm sure few remember what Rose Marie was wearing.

The once-named Northwest Mounted Police was founded in 1873 to police the Northwest Territories, whose aborigines were threatened by American whiskey merchants and similar menaces to good order. In 1882 the force provided protection to the workers on the Canadian Pacific Railway. Even then, its tunic was bright red, for Canada was still a proud member of the British Empire and happy to ape the dress usages of its army. Instead of the later Stetson hat, the unit wore a silly little bell-boy's cap with chin strap. In 1904 King Edward VII was so pleased with these mounted troops that he bestowed on them the term "Royal," and in 1974, the RCMP went so far as to enlist women. Sadly, it wears the Nelson Eddy uniform now only for ceremonial or theatrical occasions. Normally, it operates in dark blue police uniforms or plainclothes as a federal police force focusing on passports and immigration, narcotics, customs, counterfeiting, and general border policing. Now and then at a Canadian international airport you can see prop Mounties in the classic uniform performing publicity and tourist-trade duty by smiling and looking noble. But the red uniform is now so rare, writes Emily Way in *Facts About Canada,* "that many Ontarians and Québecois have never seen it except on TV." A pity, some will think, for a uniform like that to turn into a costume, especially when so few things venture to be bright red anymore. Even many fire engines have let us down by turning white.

THE FORMER RCMP uniform is one North American effort to be compared, on aesthetic grounds, with the black German SS outfit. Another is the dress uniform of the United States Marine Corps. The marines have been intelligent enough to specify that uniform as the one to be worn by members of the recruiting staff, especially, it would appear, those working in small backward places that don't see a lot of grandeur and style. In 1942, that dress uniform worked on the uncertain nineteen-year-old Eugene B. Sledge, causing him without further consideration to join the marines. The recruiting sergeant who visited his school enticed him by appearing in an immensely desirable outfit. In his memoir *With the Old Breed,* Sledge writes that he wore "dress blue trousers, a khaki shirt, necktie, and white barracks cap," and, in addition, "his shoes had a shine the likes of which I'd never seen." (Sledge forgot only the pure white belt and the wide bright-red stripes on the light blue trousers.) One uniform element was not always noticed: the shirt and tie were clearly distinguished from the Army's by the tie's not being tucked in between the top second and third shirt buttons. A subtle distinction, to be sure, but one easily seen to suggest greater precision in the USMC, for it demands careful attention, patience, and some skill to make the visible ends of the tie come out even. The Army finesses the whole problem by tucking the uneven ends out of sight, as if refusing to play the carefulness-and-accuracy game.

In the Marine Corps appearance counts mightily, today as always. The corps insists that "no eccentricities of dress will be permitted" even in civilian clothes, and of course "the wearing of earrings by male Marines, under any circumstances, is prohibited." Likewise, when in uniform or out of it, marines must obey certain specific rules about personal grooming. "No eccentricities in the manner of wearing head, facial, or body hair will be permitted." And there's official advice presumably aimed at female marines, but nice to contemplate if aimed at all: "If worn, wigs will comply with grooming regulations."

Compared with people privileged to wear the uniforms of the USMC, soldiers in the Army must feel like the lowest schmucks, or perhaps Green Jobs, talentless leftovers and losers. How can army green compete with marine light and dark blue, red stripes down trouser legs, shiny white visor caps, dress capes lined in red silk, with white gloves, white belts, goldish buttons on dress jacket cuffs, and, for ceremonial purposes, sabers even for sergeants? One contemporary red thing that has resisted change is the marine enlisted man's sleeve chevrons on his dark green walking-out uniform. Very classy.

With all this talent for the colorful, the Marine Corps has shown admirable taste in avoiding gilt buttons on the jacket of the walking-out uniform. The buttons there, together with the lapel emblems of globe and fouled anchor, surely temptations toward showy gilding, are a tasteful black, a rare display of restraint among those who design United States military uniforms. You can almost hear some long-service marine gunnery sergeant explaining, "We are so good, we don't need no faggoty gold buttons all the time." Someone running the National Guard had better wake up and stop its soldiers from appearing on, say, Saturday mornings, wearing repellent, baggy-seated, foolishly camouflage-printed battle dress. The guard needs to learn that there is such a thing as show business, and that when military service is voluntary and competitive, rather than conscripted, attractiveness and taste pay off.

One event that has sharpened the uniform consciousness of all the services is the serious inclusion of women. Indeed, in some cases, pregnant women. The regulations governing their appearance may raise a guilty smile, but they are nonetheless appropriate and sensitive. "Maternity uniforms will be worn by pregnant Marines when the local commander determines that the standard uniforms can no longer be worn. The maternity service uniform consists of green tunic top, skirt or slacks, and khaki long or short sleeve maternity shirt. . . . The web belt will not be worn." And temporary repositioning of the buttons on the jacket is authorized. The corps thinks of everything.

Chefs in Their Whites

Among people who attend to clothing design, style, and fashion, it must be an accepted understanding that conspicuous waste of material is a way to suggest the seniority and high value of the wearer. It is here that the senior chef's needlessly tall toque and the physician's unnecessarily long white lab coat have more in common than one might suspect. Both doctor and chef are engaged, like magicians, in metamorphosis, the physician changing the ill to the well (sometimes, alas, the living to the dead) and the chef transforming nondescript organic materials into irresistible viands. Each presides over a mystery, and to perform it properly, he or she must be appropriately garbed.

In both trades, the professional grades are often indicated by uniform: medical students and residents wear short white lab coats; apprentice cooks, droopy headwear. (The law requires food handlers to cover and restrain their hair.) The proudly erect tall toque is reserved for boss chefs alone. It has its own high folklore, beginning with the old superstition that it must have one hundred pleats. If not that, at least forty-eight. (No one knows why.) Proper upkeep of the toque is important. M. Roger Fessaquet, once owner of the New York restaurant Caravelle, maintains that in the old days, when the French Line was still the way to convey him and his gourmet passengers across the Atlantic, he regularly sent back to Le Havre his toques to be washed, ironed, starched, and pleated by women skilled in the art of toque maintenance. But nowadays toques tend to be made of paper and are disposable after one wearing.

The chef's uniform remains a rare example of an aristocratic tradition that (except for the paper toque) has undergone minimal change during the last two centuries. The uniform is precisely described and proudly worn. After the white headwear, a double-breasted high-neck white cotton jacket with two rows of buttons and turn-back cuffs. Trousers are either white or a black-and-white houndstooth check. It is painful to report that some current chefs' trousers are patterned with little pictures of vegetables (onions, artichokes, peppers), revealing that the age of cute leaves its marks everywhere. Students at cooking schools, the classiest ones, wear the traditional outfit, but with the white floppy hat instead of the as yet unearned noble toque. But there is one important status detail hardly noticeable by outsiders, and it is a tiny thing. The students have plastic buttons on their jackets, while real graduate chefs' jackets fasten with white cloth knot buttons. The prices of these two styles convey a sufficient social-class message: the plastic-button jacket costs $18.00; the knot-button one, $29.98. The black-and-white check trousers are the same for both "officers" and "enlisted men." A pair costs $29.50.

This is all serious stuff, as a visitor to a school for aspirant chefs soon discovers. One of the few variables permitted the students is the trousers, which, given the likelihood of student spills, may even be blue jeans. But above the waist, no variations, please. A white napkin knotted around the neck is usually not worn when the student is actually cooking, but it is useful for the top chef to add drama and class if an audience is watching, or during the occasional tour of the dining room to solicit the congratulations of the customers.

Just like the physician's white coat, the white chef's uniform suggests standards of obsessive cleanliness, regardless of the occasional facts, nicely projected in the subversive restaurant kitchen scenes in George Orwell's *Down and Out in Paris and London*. Of one stylish restaurant where he worked as a dishwasher, he writes, "The kitchen grew dirtier and the rats bolder, though we trapped a few of them. Looking round that filthy room, with raw meat lying among refuse on the floor, clotted saucepans sprawling everywhere, and the sink blocked and coated with grease, I used to wonder whether there could be a restaurant in the world as bad as ours." But three of Orwell's kitchen mates "all said that they had seen dirtier places." Orwell, a well-known master of exaggeration, concludes, "I shall never again . . . enjoy a meal at a smart restaurant."

The white of the chef's kitchen uniform certainly goes some way to counterbalance several of Orwell's details. But one still wonders, Why all the white?

Not to press the similarity too far, some may recall the term "whitewings," applied to the men garbed all in white, with brooms, shovels, and wheeled refuse cans, who used to follow parades in the Old World, dealing with the horse dung. Their white suggested that there must be something immaculate about what they were doing and that they were almost scientifically indispensable to public health.

The Nurses' Revolt

If you're close to sixty, have a good memory, and have spent a bit of time in a large hospital (which God forbid), you may have noticed something strange. In a hospital recently, I was struck by a memorable oddity. The nurses appeared not in their traditional uniform (white shoes and hose, white dress, all-important starched white cap, and navy blue cape for out-doors), but dressed any old way, including blue jeans, as if they were ashamed of any sign of education or distinction, let alone simple identification. The impulse may have been a desire to fit in with the floor moppers and trash collectors and not be recognized as trained professionals, members of a formerly proud sorority. This novel phenomenon struck me as misguided, when, as a bed patient, I wanted to see a nurse now and then and the only caregivers I could raise looked like charladies.

Schools of nursing have long been aware of their students' unhappiness with the white uniform, especially the cap. Thus the disuse of the former "capping" ceremony at graduation and its replacement by a "pinning" ceremony. There's an interesting dilemma connected with the nurses' uniform problem. Two equally powerful opposite forces may be at work. One is the impulse to wear the easily recognized standard uniform, grati-fying the instinct to show off as a member of an honored seg-ment of society. The other is the impulse not to appear formally identified as a subordinate, a servant to a higher class, namely, physicians. One might just as well be a maid or a waitress.

There's a valuable thing the nurses abandon when they give up the white uniform, and that is the opportunity to have, in red embroidered script above the left breast, their name and their academic degree and often their medical specialty, as do physicians. Ultimately the nurses may allow instinctive human vanity to lead them back to a form of dress that permits them to brag a bit, and in handsome red script.

The nursing profession has a very short history. It began in Prussia around the 1830s. Prussia, as the Nazis demonstrated, was a place where the message conveyed by one's attire was crucial. It was the site of the first nurses' training school, founded and administered by Theodor and Friedericke Fliedner, who realized that in an authoritarian society, where women without visible husbands were generally scorned, nursing could not pass the respectability test unless a uniform came to its assistance, convincing onlookers that these young women were not whores or otherwise up to no good. The Fliedners' uniform had to be different from the gloomy black ensemble worn by Catholic nursing sisters. They settled on a dark blue, floor-length dress with a blue cotton apron, a white collar with a white ribbon closure, and a white bonnet that tied under the chin. No trim or frivolity was allowed, and the whole get-up spoke of sobriety, sexlessness, dignity, and "professionalism."

Once "germs" were discovered, white garb, when worn in the vicinity of the sick, gave the appearance of being sterile, and that useful delusion has persisted almost to the present moment, when green or blue operating-room attire has become mandatory in hospitals and chic on the sidewalks outside. One suggestion from nurses who don't like the old uniform but who don't want to look like the cleaning women is a conspicuous badge reading RN. But hospitals have objected, believing that patients (increasingly called clients) would then know who is a nurse and who is not, and feel cheated when assigned a nurse visibly not qualified.

Increasingly popular among nurses are white trousers worn under a baggy white lab coat, useful for its large pockets to hold thermometers, stethoscopes, sphygmomanometers (blood-pressure measuring apparatus), and other necessities. White is the favorite color for a reformed uniform, but no one has yet suggested that operating-room nurses wear blood-red lab coats to hide stains. One medical-dress uniform manufacturer does offer a special uniform for nurses fearful of spurting fluids. It provides "fluid-proof protection," and we all know what the euphemism is hiding.

PERHAPS THE EASIEST solution to the nurses' uniform problem would be long white lab coats for all, with red script identification.

In a recent appointment with a doctor, I was shocked to find him out of uniform, wearing a tweed jacket and khakis. I felt both uncertain of the roles we were playing and a bit annoyed at being cheated.

Little Sailor Suits

In nontotalitarian countries, at least, children seldom wear uniforms associated with military service. To be sure, one does occasionally see pictures of boys whose fathers were in the army or navy in World War II wearing cute tiny army uniforms run up by mothers and friends on their sewing machines. (Unsurprisingly, the child is usually costumed as an officer.) And today it's possible to see children playing happily in battle-dress camouflage outfits, not knowing yet what that uniform can imply. But from the middle of the nineteenth century until well into the twentieth, so many boys wore identical sailor suits as to make that style a uniform, despite the knee pants.

It all began in Britain, where, around 1846, Queen Victoria dressed her sons in little dark blue suits, making them look like midget members of the Royal Navy. And the custom endured for a century, ending only when the Empire began to break up. The boy's sailor suit was always a highly conservative uniform, strongly suggestive of at least upper-middle-class status. At the time, the British navy was one of the most respected institutions in the world, cementing, on its cruises and port visits, the most extensive and powerful empire since antiquity. For a small boy to appear in a sailor suit was to suggest that his family was on the political right side and to signal that he was probably familiar with a certain amount of privilege and discipline.

The standard version of the uniform, made of navy blue

wool, had a middy blouse with rectangular naval collar over the shoulders, short pants, silk neckerchief, and as much pseudo-authentic naval décor as would suffice to thrill the wearer: embroidered badges of rank, whistle with white lanyard, and more. The sailor suit was popular well outside Britain. In fact, one could find boys wearing it all over Europe. The ten-year-old Tadzio, object of Aschenbach's obsession in Thomas Mann's *Death in Venice,* despite being Polish, was correctly dressed in the uniform. "He wore an English sailor suit, with quilted sleeves, . . . breast knot, lacings, and embroideries."

Accessories like the silver whistle were common in boys' clothing of the 1920s and 1930s. When one bought a major bit of clothing, one was likely to receive a "prize." Boys' shoes with sharkskin toes, held to be scuff-proof, sold themselves by presenting a real shark's tooth with each pair.

The popularity of the sailor collar in Japanese and Korean girls' school uniforms sufficiently suggests obedience, like the collar on the white sailor jumpers, which are the uniform of the Vienna Boy's Choir, founded in 1498. In Europe, formal wear for boys was likely to be the all-white version, with high white stockings and white shoes.

The reasons for the rise and fall of boys' sailor suits invite speculation. Such a uniform would hardly be popular in a society valuing freedom and "creativeness." The perfect setting for the sailor suit was the Kipling period. It would not be attractive in a country whose armed forces cannot keep natives in check, or stock its armed forces with manpower except by, say, costly and mendacious advertising.

Addendum on Sloppery

And clearly the sailor suit could not trace its true home to a country like ours, which goes in for a widespread concept of uniform usage best described as "sloppery." This tendency was noted by most Europeans who saw American soldiers in the

Second World War and were astonished by their apparent sloppiness, in contrast with continental military norms.

The ten-year-old John Keegan, later a war historian, was enraptured by the sloppery of the GIs swarming in England before the Normandy invasion — leaning against buildings, adopting a comfortable rather than a military posture, driving their jeeps with one leg outside, foot on the fender, and, if possible, steering ostentatiously with one hand. The war correspondent Ernie Pyle saw U.S. soldiers as unique because "we admittedly are not a rigid-minded people. . . . Our boys sing in the streets, unbutton their shirt collars, laugh and shout and forget to salute." (*Forget to* was probably too kind; *refuse to* would have been more accurate.)

For all this, we could invoke a designation like "Huck Finnery" or "the Conscript's Revenge." Conscious sloppery was a way of saying, "I'm not really a powerless part of an institution so unfair, stupid, and silly as the Army. I'm still the careless boy from Winnetka that I used to be, and I am determined forever to be my own boss. Screw you all."

Uniforming the Scouts and Others

Before the Boy Scouts there was the Boys Brigade, the idea of a Sunday school teacher in Glasgow, William Smith. In 1883 he started a boys' nature-study group based on religion and discipline, for which he devised routines of drill and gymnastics. At first, the uniform consisted of badge, cap, haversack, and belt. As the idea was finally exported to sixty countries, the uniform grew more serious and soon added blue shirt and trousers with a small blue cap to match. Smith's idea rapidly found imitators, and soon there were the Church Lads Brigade, Boys Life Brigade, Jewish Lads Brigade, Catholic Boys Brigade, and Girls Life Brigade. Smith's Boys Brigade is still going on, its religious element derived from the beliefs of the Church of Scotland, and some of its boys' pipe bands still wear kilts.

By the time General Robert Baden-Powell founded the Boy Scouts, in 1908, the idea of uniformed youth may have become rather tired, but Baden-Powell, a celebrated hero of the Boer War, brought new emphasis to the military component while diluting the religious element toward a mild deism. For Baden-Powell, the word "scout" carried distinctly military connotations, for in late-nineteenth-century armies, scouts had the job of secretly observing the enemy and inferring his condition and plans. The early uniforms of Baden-Powell's scouts, then, were difficult to distinguish, in many respects, from those of real British troops. The khaki-colored wool tunic rose to a high collar and buttoned all the way up between four flap pockets, but the buttons displayed not the army but the Scout emblem. Baden-Powell once declared of the uniform that it was "an important item, not merely an attraction, as it undoubtedly was to girls, but because under it all differences of social standing were hidden and forgotten." The language of scouting quite betrayed its military bent: a regulated group of Scouts took the designation "troop" from the cavalry, and each troop consisted of various "patrols," each of them with a guidon on a pole, aping the military lance. Scout troops endured rigorous inspections, and there was lots of saluting and standing at attention. Indeed, the Scouts' pseudo-military behavior prompted many to conceive of it as a junior branch of the Territorial Army, the British equivalent of the American National Guard.

Christopher Wagner, an authority on the Scout uniform, writes, "The early American Scout uniform followed the English example, but with some relaxations. The English and some Europeans give great attention to the uniform, more so than in the more easygoing United States. . . . In America, Scouting is much more identified with outdoor events where uniform standards were less rigorous."

In the United States, the main effort has been an enthusiastic demilitarizing of the uniform. The broad-brimmed hat, suggestive of the camp wear of First World War conscripts, is no longer official, nor are breeches, now replaced by trousers or shorts. The neckerchief, perhaps the main Scout distinction, remains, with its fancy slide. Correct neckerchiefs and slides were regarded as very important at a typical International Scout Jamboree, a former Scout noted. "There was lots of trading of slides, and the neckerchief indicated what district you were from, sort of a geographical roadmap."

As with nuns and nurses, not to mention employees enjoying the casual days recognized by many businesses, there has been a significant easing of uniform rigor everywhere. And now in America, as Wagner emphasizes, "Scout troops are allowed considerable leeway on how to wear the uniform, and over the years a great diversity of hats, kerchiefs, knickers, long and short pants, can be observed in Scout troops." Some Scouts show up at troop meetings in blue jeans, with only a neckerchief (often with a rubber band for a slide) to indicate their Scouthood. It is not hard to imagine the founder's horror could he have known of this recent official ruling: "The main component of a Boy Scout 'Class B' uniform is a Scout T-shirt." Adolescent boys are naturally subversive, and Baden-Powell's initial motive may have been to impose some order on these instinctively skeptical, socially dangerous children. The apparent strength of the American anti-uniform impulse suggests that American adolescent males may be more threatening than those of other countries.

Despite the Scouts' long-term movement toward demilitarizing, during the height of the Cold War, on the rare occasions when Scouts wore the complete uniform, a small patch depicting the American flag appeared on the shirt's right shoulder, and some army touches were seen, like overseas caps and trousers bloused over leggings. The temptation to militarize is always there, as can be inferred from the official voice cautioning, "The Boy Scouts are not a military unit. Camouflage attire is not permitted."

So far, the Girl Scouts, initially called the Girl Guides and led by Baden-Powell's sister Agnes, have avoided the militaristic temptation, although they have committed other sins against the nonbellicose dignified uniform look. At the beginning of their movement, the girls wore navy blue, and when blue dye grew scarce during the Great War, adopted khaki, although in its day khaki was regarded as too military for females. The Girl Scouts' recent changes in uniform have been intended to supersede the plainness, if not the downright ugliness, of the familiar gray-green dress, worn from 1928 to 1968. (My wife donated hers to the Smithsonian, where it was gladly received and is exhibited from time to time, especially on the birthday of Juliette Gordon Low, founder of the American branch in 1912.)

Today, the one-piece dress is out, and the word is "separates," and what separates they are: cargo trousers with external pockets of the sort soldiers used for carrying boxes of K-rations; khaki shorts; floppy brimmed bucket hats. "You can't even tell they're Girl Scouts," commented one of the faithful, but they are, given their vests and the shoulder sashes displaying merit and other badges. The whole new outfit seems to have been designed by a permanent chaperon as an absolute antidote to anything like affection.

The organization has done what it can with the style and charm of its junior division, stuck with the name Brownies, but it still leans toward brown shirts and knee-high brown shorts and brown beanies. For leaders and older members there are attractive navy two-piece suits, trouser suits, shorts, blouses, and a variety of handsome scarves. But the trouble now is that the audience is unaware that these good-looking Bill Blass outfits identify a branch of the Girl Scouts. Brownies have never enjoyed the advantage of Norman Rockwell's blazoning their uniformed image all over the country, and always in aid of a noble, or at least a sentimental, message. One Girl Scout leader, Ann Bilbrey, typically testified:

> My two troops marched in the Memorial Day parade. . . .
> It was interesting to watch the boys march too. All had
> their shirt and scarf. The packs had their banners with
> over thirty years of ribbons flying in the breeze. . . . They
> were an impressive sight. As the main group of girls passed
> by, people would spare them a glance — some would clap
> — you could hear an occasional "Who are they?" from
> the crowd. We were at the end of the line of Girl Scouts
> and when we came by you heard "There's the Girl
> Scouts!" and clapping. There were about twenty girls of
> my two troops there. But when the boys came by (over a
> hundred) all in uniform with their banner proudly fluttering
> in the breeze, you would hear a lot more clapping and
> the "Wow! Look at that banner!" Mostly what we heard
> was recognition. The lay person in the crowd saw those
> boys in their uniform — pretty much the same uniform
> they had seen in paintings and ads since the early 1900s —
> and *recognized* them. So there you are — one small experience
> in wearing a uniform. Overall, there were more

girls than boys marching in that Memorial Day parade, but all those people saw were these boys wearing their uniforms.

But in seeking an explanation, Ann Bilbrey perhaps paid too little attention to the occasion: Memorial Day. Maybe the boys in their khakis and neckerchiefs brought to mind their possible future usefulness as cannon fodder in a way the girls did not. You can go some way toward demilitarizing the Boy Scout uniform, but it's harder to demilitarize the crowd.

IF THE Girl Scouts' uniform is not widely recognized, the uniform of what used to be known as the Camp Fire Girls may be even less familiar, and the organization doesn't make recognition easier by changing its name from time to time. It began in 1910 and admitted boys (now 46 percent of the membership) in 1975, when it renamed itself Camp Fire Boys and Girls. In the year 2001 it renamed itself again, this time to Camp Fire USA, which will surely prevent its being widely useful outside the United States. That would be a pity, for it is devoted largely to societal good works — racial integration, social responsibility, and "improving conditions in society which have an impact on children."

Red, white, and blue are the colors of the Camp Fire uniform. Boys may wear blue trousers, white shirt, and blue open vest; girls, blue skirts and red vest. On the vests appear patches indicating achievements and awards. On the vest you can show that you've participated in "Salute to Hospitalized Veterans" or the "Save the Bluebirds" campaign. There's a badge for "Nature Awareness" as well as for "Community Government." If you were to hang around the Camp Fire Boys and Girls long enough and look at their vests a lot, you could learn a great deal about children — what they're proud of, and what their position in the world can be.

Women's Nuptial Uniform

In addition to virtually inventing the boy's sailor suit, Queen Victoria may be credited with the popularity of the white wedding gown. Before her marriage to Prince Albert, in 1840, wedding dresses came in all colors. Her wedding gown established not just the proper color of the gown but its association with virginity. Over the years the design of the gown has remained astonishingly unchanged, at least in its basic elements. There is the white satin and the white lace, and the tulle veil attached to a "crown," and a train varying in length from a foot or so to a monster twenty-five feet, so heavy that a staff of handlers is required to manage it. The ensemble is frequently finished off with white lace gloves, plus a white lace hanky to be held wadded up in one hand. The other hand must clutch the indispensable bouquet, once regarded as a fertility symbol, as was the rice thrown at the happy couple as they depart for a good time. The predominance of white has tempted some wits to offer explanations, like that of the fashion writer Barbara Tober: "Victorian brides from privileged backgrounds wore white to indicate that they were rich enough to wear a dress for one day only."

Before long, white was so well established as correct that one poetaster could award it first place in a survey of wedding colors:

Married in white, you have chosen all right.
Married in gray, you will go far away.
Married in black, you will wish yourself back.
Married in red, you will wish yourself dead.
Married in green, ashamed to be seen.
Married in yellow, ashamed of your fellow.
Married in pink, your fortune will sink.

But every institution has its Zumwalts, and in the wedding gown trade there is now a movement toward "surprising touches of color, everything from the palest of pinks to the deepest crimson." As one professional gown furnisher says, "The look is fresh, exciting, and — dare we say it? — welcome in an industry where white weddings prevail and a general lack of color has become commonplace."

Merchandisers of wedding gowns are a specialist branch of the fashion trade, and they tend to divide the bride's choices of styles between "Body conscious and Sexy" on the one hand and, on the other, "Return to the Classics," which implies the chaste look. Features like halters, sleevelessness, and strapless are thought sexy, and so are low-cut backs. A peek-a-boo, almost strip-tease effect can be engineered by providing a transparent overlay for a traditional sexless gown.

As everyone knows who has been through the wedding trauma, the industry must be taken seriously. The gown today costs well over $500, the veil alone around $100. And there are the sums exacted by the printer of the invitations and announcements, the florist, the photographer, the musicians, the limousine (with chauffeur) providers, the reception caterers, and the clergy.

The object is to create an unforgettable moment. To prolong and preserve it, another group of specialists among wedding consultants may be called in to "embalm" the wedding gown and turn it into a relic. To bring this about, the bride and her family are enjoined to, first, commit the gown to a professional dry cleaner, who will remove wine and fruit juice stains and check for loose pearls, threads, and buttons. The next event will be what the trade calls "heirlooming." This involves storing the gown on a hanger in a heavy plastic bag or — the more costly method — wrapping it in acid-free tissue in a vacuum-sealed archival box ("Air is an enemy of longevity"). This will cost from $115 to $150. Crucial is the likely humidity where bag or box is stored. Ideal temperature is 65, ideal humidity 48 percent. And there should be no fluorescent light, because it tends to destroy silk. As storage places, wooden dressers and cedar chests should be avoided, because wood gives off gases and is highly acidic.

John Lappe, the owner of the Museum Quality Storage Box Company and Preservation Service in Pleasantville, New York, points out that "people who spend a lot of money on a wedding dress are interested in preserving it, but generally only first wedding dresses are preserved as heirlooms." Mr. Lappe's experience has taught him that Jews and Italians are the most interested in bridal gown preservation, and that New York and California are where most preservationist clients live. With two and a half million full-dress weddings a year, preserving women's most significant uniform has become a big business, like the divorce industry.

Broad-Brimmed Hats

In a contest to name the most admired nonmilitary uniformed service of the United States, the winner would probably be a toss-up between the letter carriers of the Postal Service and the rangers of the National Park Service, the only men and women (marine drill instructors excepted) who can wear the broad-brimmed Stetson hat without risking ridicule. Indeed, they wear that hat with pride and dignity, as we shall see, even though some women Rangers complain that it messes up their hair. That hat's silent allusion to the similar headwear traditionally associated with the Royal Canadian Mounted Police does no harm to the rangers' reputation for trustworthiness and courtesy.

The first National Park was Yellowstone, so designated in 1872. It soon became clear that someone had to keep visitors from teasing the animals and from spoiling the romantic setting with discarded candy wrappers and soft-drink bottles. These guardians were first called "scouts," and since the U.S. Army was initially in charge of this park and the many others to follow, each scout wore a military uniform or a silvery badge. Military usage prevailed, the scouts being divided into officers and men. The officers got to wear a silver badge; the men, a nickel-plated one. Over the years the scouts came to be called rangers, and their force, a bureau governed by the Department of the Interior since 1920, grew increasingly egalitarian, which may help to explain its popularity. It is now a uniformed force, one that signifies some of the best things about the United States.

It was only when the National Park Service came under the aegis of the Department of the Interior that the park rangers were uniformed according to a national standard and arguments began. One important question was how military these people ought to look. Should their jacket buttons be the same as those on soldiers' uniforms? Or should they involve images of pine trees? Throughout the history of the Park Service the button question has surfaced repeatedly, until now the buttons show the eagle from the national coat of arms but in a less bellicose, more relaxed and conservationist pose. Over the years button reformers have considered Sequoia pines and pine cones, bisons and snow-covered mountain tops, all of which appear on the service's shoulder patch in the form of an arrowhead.

The National Park Service divides its uniformed members into interpreters and protectors. The interpreters explain things and answer questions. They wear the snazzy green uniform. The protection staff, seen less often, is a police force whose members are armed with pistols and trained to handle emergencies, like medical rescues and fires. Both wear the hat, with its unique leather band displaying embossed images of pines and pine cones. That hatband is one of the most remarkable bits of folk art and affectation we have.

Rangers are given an annual allowance of $400 for their uniforms. The beautiful dark green jackets and trousers do not often need replacing, for they are soundly made. The service is extremely conscious of threats to the integrity of the uniform and its insignia. Counterfeiting, selling, or possessing the shoulder patch without authorization, for example, will cost the malefactor a fine and imprisonment. The uniform consciousness of the service can be appreciated from the elaborate administrative machinery connected with that uniform. A service-wide uniform manager coordinates the entire program and supervises seven regional uniform managers. He also pays attention to the recommendations of five advisory groups, required to

meet together every other year. All this administration is necessary because of the complexities. The service recognizes three
standard uniforms. The service uniform is worn by virtually all
rangers who have contact with the public. The field uniform,
less formal, is worn, says the official manual, "by employees engaged in visitor contact activities in situations where the Service Uniform would be impractical or inappropriate due to cli-
mate, terrain, or safety." And, finally, the work uniform is worn
by those in back-stage operations, like taking out the garbage
or trimming trees, or activities requiring special clothing, like
welding or working with barbed wire or firefighting.

But it is the forest-green service uniform that is indispensable in maintaining high public respect for the rangers, and, as
the official manual says, "The ranger hat is worn wherever possible." It comes in both winter (felt) and summer (straw) versions. And of course there's a maternity model of the service
uniform, featuring adjustable black trousers. Even the bathing
attire of service lifeguards is attended to: on trunks or swim
suits, the Park Service emblem (the arrowhead) must appear.
The regulations are eminently specific. A brass name bar must
be worn over the right jacket pocket. "Every name bar must include the employee's full last name and first name or first initials. Name bars never contain titles such as 'Mr.,' 'Mrs.,' 'Dr.,'
or 'Ph.D.'" On the jacket the ranger wears a gold-plated badge
of tasteful, that is, modest, size, and it "must shine." A dupli-
cate badge is issued for attaching to the light gray shirt when it
is worn without the jacket, to save the ranger from constantly
changing insignia from one bit of clothing to another. That is
certainly a thoughtful idea, although some of the regulations
may go too far. Like: "Sunglasses may be worn with uniforms,
but sunglasses that are dark enough to make it difficult or impossible to see the employee's eyes should be worn in visitor
contact situations only when absolutely necessary. Mirrored
sunglasses are prohibited."

Rangers may sometimes feel that they're really in the armed
services: "All buttons are to be buttoned." "Shirts should always be . . . 'bloused,' where the shirt is gathered at the sides or

in back and tucked in so that the front is smooth." And there's even attention to the gig line: "A straight line should be maintained through the shirt buttons, belt buckle, and fly." Obesity is not allowed, which is the tenor of the message sent by "waistbands on pants should not roll outward." The light green raincoat "must be worn only fully zipped or fully opened," and it may be worn "only when it is precipitating." (When it is *what?*)

Grooming is strictly regulated. Men are forbidden to wear earrings and nail polish. "Beards no longer than two inches in length are permitted. Beards must be long enough to indicate that the beard is intentional rather than giving the appearance that the wearer has been negligent in shaving." And there are rules covering behavior while one is uniformed. Drinking alcohol and smoking or chewing tobacco in public view are forbidden, and so are gambling in any form and being seen to sleep when on duty. And enough of the early military mode remains to require rangers to be proficient in saluting and in standing at attention and parade rest.

The unique hat is so important that a whole section of the manual is devoted to its proper wear and upkeep. "The ranger hat is the most important, recognized, and respected symbol associated with the National Park Service, and it should be worn with pride and care." Care means worn straight across, without the levity of tip-back or "canting" (tipping sideways), and "no hair may hang below the brim on the wearer's forehead." (That's the way the Navy insists the white gob's hat be worn, but it has learned how hard it is to enforce that rule.)

And, finally, there are principles governing "burial in uniform." "In the case of line-of-duty death, the Service encourages the family to consider this method of burial, which is allowed with full collar brass and badge."

Just to enter the language precincts of these loyal custodians of the right attitude toward the outdoors is already to smell the pine trees and be conveyed back a century and more to the launching of America's formal love affair with romantic nature, immersion in which is conceived as magically good for you and worth perpetual care by the NPS.

Civilian Uniformities

Brandi Barhite, writing in the magazine *Hotel and Motel Management,* emphasizes that in that trade, employees' uniforms must do more than simply identify their wearers as belonging. They must elevate and sustain morale, for she knows that, quietly, everyone really likes to appear in a uniform — better than trying to make it on your own and risk failure. "Building self-esteem" is the object. One uniform manufacturer says, "If employees feel they look good in their uniforms, then they will feel good about themselves." Likewise, Marc Ellin, of the Grand Hyatt Hotel in Washington, observes, "We take uniforms seriously. We like employees to like what they are wearing."

Just as employees like to wear uniforms, sentimental and egalitarian vaporings to the contrary, so does everyone, even if their civilian uniforms are less obvious and seldom so designated. Anne Hollander, the historian of clothing, accurately perceives that "uniforms, so vigorously despised in much current rhetoric about clothes, are really what most people prefer to wear." Erving Goffman's writings imply the universal human sense of imminent ridicule or rejection lying in wait for anyone venturing unconventionally into public view. That is to recognize that most people are to some degree frightened all the time. Dressing approximately like others is to don armor against contempt. Better to be not noticed at all than noticed and targeted as odd. Wearers of colorful tights are simply asking for it — and they deserve little sympathy, as everyone knows.

A memorable example of this principle is Private Robert E. Lee Prewitt, in James Jones's *From Here to Eternity*. He sticks with the peacetime Army despite its ill treatment of him because he is quintessentially lonely. He longs to belong to "the comp'ny," no matter how defective, to achieve security and safety. When in the Army's official unprepossessing dirt-dyed, if not excrement-colored, uniform, he feels safe, and when out of that uniform, among civilians in Honolulu, he is careful to appear in another sort of uniform, the colorful "Hawaiian" shirt, rigorously worn outside the trousers, and never tucked in. Everyone wears that in Hawaii and, thus oddly attired, avoids being stared at or considered an oddball. Harry Truman used to startle expectation by wearing a loud Hawaiian shirt on his vacations in Key West. It made him a target of mockery, for he should have been wearing a less raucous resort uniform, better suited to his age and position.

Harry Truman was an extraordinary person, because he was obviously secure in his unpretentious identity, which doubtless annoyed many people. And a little consideration of actual instead of apparent motives will reveal the predominance of simple loneliness as a motivator of the quest for uniformity. W. H. Auden's remark about homosexuals in general sheds some light on the grouping impulse: "We're all about eleven years old emotionally." Noticing the popularity of T-shirts and sweatshirts bearing mottoes, injunctions, and, pre-eminently, brand names and advertisements, Alison Lurie coined the useful term Legible Clothing. The journalist Christopher Wagner commented, "The meaning of the desire of boys and girls to serve as living billboards is difficult to assess." But not if one notices how lonely the young are, without firm and respectable groupings to hide their individuality in. And even when they grow up, these boys and girls assuage their loneliness by becoming joiners — of churches and synagogues, bridge clubs, fraternal lodges, alumni groups, political parties, and veterans' associations — to a degree that astonishes Europeans.

Rabid sports fans, who identify their teams' successes with their own psychological well-being, have been examined by the journalist James C. McKinley Jr., who noted that fans see teams as extensions of themselves, providing a form of "comp'ny" that helps to mitigate loneliness and insignificance. One psychologist observed that a fan of a winning team will say, "We won," and a fan of a losing team will say, "They lost." It has even been observed that male fans of winning teams, in their exultation, actually experience an increase in testosterone level. Another psychologist finds that "the desire to belong to a group or society — a need once fulfilled mostly by religious and political organizations — may explain why some fans remain loyal despite the repeated failure of their teams." And some rabid fans identify themselves so intimately with their teams that an injury to a player sends them to bed. One fan reports of such an occasion, "I was sick to my stomach. I was sick that day." A female fan of the New York Knicks confirms that her "twenty-seven-year love affair with the team may have had its genesis in loneliness," after her husband ran away with the woman next door.

Anyone familiar with the magazines given out on airplanes could easily conclude that the corporate classes, especially the junior-grade members, are equally desperate not to appear socially alone. How else to interpret the presence of costly advertisements offering to equip readers with a "Harvard Graduate's Vocabulary in just 15 minutes a day"? And for only $34.90 you can acquire two tapes delivering the secrets of conversation practiced by the enviable members of groups that are socially secure. But to those still conscious of their risky individuality, irony lurks in these presentations of group happiness. Speaking of women and their unremitting pursuit of "beauty," the *New York Times* columnist Maureen Dowd enunciated a home truth: "Instead of broadening the choices of how to look good, we have only broadened the way we try to look alike: we spend

$8 billion a year on an infinite number of creams designed to make us conformists with perfect complexions."

DESPITE SOME RELAXATION of rigor, it remains true that the dark business suit (or its female equivalent) is still close to obligatory, at least in businesses that have little truck with novelty, like serious law, most banks, and the upper reaches of the securities markets. The well-advertised dress-down or casual Friday has, of course, managed to impose its own uniform conventions; no worker would venture to appear in anything like colored tights or, in torrid weather, swim suits, or in really sexy micro-miniskirts. One dresses down only to join the club defined by what others are wearing — even in California, the home of every-day casual, with jeans and khakis almost insisted upon. But women have a longer list of casual *don'ts* than men have: no shorts, no low-cut tank tops, no Capri pants, no spandex fabrics ("too skin-tight"). No sneakers or thongs, and some offices frown on open-toed sandals. No gym clothes or "picnic outfits."

Going about the office barefoot is rare, but it has been done. The practice of not wearing a bra is spreading, like not wearing any possible thing utilizing a stretch fabric. Shorts for both sexes are common, although people who have to impress clients with their dignity — funeral directors, for example, or presidents of ancient universities — can never wear such things on duty. It all depends on what you're selling: Silicon Valley has a markedly different uniform code from, say, the Episcopal church. In progressive venues, work-out wear and jogging outfits may be worn on casual days, as long as they are chaste. But even work-out wear must be purged of all elements of originality, lest the wearer risk the appearance of someone not entirely belonging.

Some businesses have tried to take a middle-of-the-road position, designating their ideal for dress-down days as "business casual." One social adviser explains that ideal by recommending for men a standard civilian uniform: "You can't go wrong with the classic navy blue blazer and khakis." (That is, incidentally, the uniform I wear all the time to stay out of sartorial trouble.) This ensemble has become a uniform because it is favored above all others by men in the armed forces when they appear in civilian clothes. Sometimes, when Senate business has to be enacted on a weekend, some senators venture to appear in the civilian uniform of the retired military officer, blazer and beige trousers, but, the weekend over, it's back to the dark suit with white shirt and unnoticeable tie. And some who work at home by computer and are never publicly visible continue to dress up for their act, reporting that they "feel more professional."

One thing universal in the dress-down uniform movement is the repudiation of the time-honored, all-but-sacred necktie. One progressive executive went all the way, proclaiming, "If you wear a tie, you shouldn't be in the Internet business." The tie, as a reactionary object, is termed by some radicals "the business noose," and it is capable of moving some informal uniform enthusiasts to violence. The *Wall Street Journal* wrote of one New York business consultant who (presumably on a Friday) received in his office a visitor wearing a necktie. Quick as a flash, he whipped out a pair of scissors and snipped off the visitor's tie. The snipper did feel some compassion, however, and offered the victim $20 for the damage, but warned, "Don't you ever wear a tie in my office again."

The canonical authority on the necktie as a compulsory element of the serious civilian uniform is John T. Molloy, the author of *Dress for Success* (1975). An admirable empiricist, Molloy loves to set up social experiments and then sit back and record the results. Once, for example, he wanted to test the principle that responsible men worth hiring for desirable jobs wear neckties. He had a series of people interviewed for good jobs. Some wore ties; others did not. "Invariably," he found, "those men who wore their ties to interviews were offered jobs; those without them were turned down. And in one almost incredible situation, the interviewer . . . was made so uncomfortable by the applicant's lack of a tie that he gave the man $6.50, told him to go out, buy a tie, put it on, and then come back to complete the interview." That man still didn't get the job, having given evidence of his lack of judgment.

In another of Molloy's experiments, he positioned himself at the Port Authority Bus Terminal in New York City, posing as a man who had to get back to his home in the suburbs but had left his wallet at home. During the rush hours he tried to borrow seventy-five cents for his bus fare, the first hour wearing a suit but no tie, the second hour properly uniformed, tie and all. "In the first hour," he reports, "I made $7.23, but in the second, with my tie on, I made $26, and one man even gave me extra money for a newspaper."

Needless to say, the dress-down movement has been terrible for manufacturers of suits and the whole tailoring trade. The journalist Sherri Day writes on a leading Wall Street men's clothing establishment: "Gone are the tailors, who once numbered 30 and performed free alterations. The sewing room is now dark, with the machines pushed against the wall and boxes stacked in the middle of the floor. There are no shoes for sale. Even the longtime phone number has been disconnected." And the *Philadelphia Inquirer* reports, "The irrepressible spread of casual dress at work from Fridays to every day of the week is forcing Pincus Bros. Inc., Philadelphia's last major men's clothing maker, to close its factory. . . . Thirty-five years ago, Philadelphia manufactured more clothing than any other U.S. city. Botany 500 suits, After Six formal wear, and Good Lad Children's Clothing are among the names that have disappeared from the Philadelphia manufacturing landscape." One can only hope that Pincus Brothers has fled in a southerly direction, perhaps to Central America, where suits are still worn (Argentina?) and wages are enticingly low.

NOW, TO TURN from the mass production of jackets and trousers to the rare one-at-a-time delicacies of artistic culture. Because literature and genuine art are not produced by committees, writers of some intellectual substance have been chary of groups. They have gone so far as to stigmatize self-conscious groups as enemies of culture — their kind of culture, the kind absorbed by silent individuals reading alone. It can be said that some elements of the struggle against uniformity lie at the heart of most modern cultural artifacts of quality. Hard to imagine James Joyce, say, associating his imaginative efforts with a group.

Certainly one legacy of the early-nineteenth-century Romantic movement is the intense celebration of the individual, no matter what the cost. The general European adulation of Lord Byron is an example. In the wings, waiting to enter, was the corollary social opposition to the group's pretensions to virtue and its suspicions of originality. The Nazi movement to a degree explained itself as an attempt to restore to authenticity and high value the idea of the group.

In opposition, the idea of the precious individual resonates all through modernist writing. Joyce's Stephen Dedalus says fervently, "I go to forge in the smithy of my soul the uncreated conscience of my race." Not, notice, *We* and *our souls*. There, the group to be escaped from is the Irish lower middle class, with its attendant priests and alcoholism. The British aesthete Cyril Connolly designates the enemy as "Group Man," a particular menace in an era of expanding mass production. In his book of meditations and aphorisms *The Unquiet Grave* (1944), Connolly draws the outline of a "magic" circle, designating it "a charm against the group man." The circle suggestively demarcates the French area of Périgord, with its elite delights of truffles, solid, traditional architecture, and various examples of natural and unnatural beauty of an ancient kind. Similarly notable, for all the differences between European and American understanding, was Lionel Trilling's disinclination to become a Group Man by joining the leftist political groups soliciting his intellectual support and validation in the 1930s and 1940s.

During his seven years at the Charterhouse School in England, the poet Robert Graves had to test his powerful — some thought simply nutty — individuality against the equally powerful group idea. He faced the same circumstance in the army in the First World War. There, he was considered a "rotten outsider," who, as one of his acquaintances said, "always manages to do things differently from other people." This streak of singularity never weakened, and after the war, he spent most of his remaining life in Majorca, conspicuously outside the groups called "England" and "normal English society."

ONE LOOKS ABOUT and perceives that the Group Man has undeniably won. No one could fail to perceive that, and many would doubtless applaud it, having experienced the uniformity visible on any major highway. The success of duplicated outcrops of the same unoriginal fast-food establishments suggests, like nothing else, the popular need for the reassurance of uniformity. But as the art historian Karal Ann Marling writes, "When the naysayers decry the sameness of the cultural landscape of fast food, they miss the point. Every White Castle or McDonald's constitutes a kind of clean, well-lighted place, an oasis of familiarity and reassurance amid the uncertainties of life along the Interstate."

Human beings are the only species with minds complicated enough to trap themselves in the paradox of uniforms: each person senses the psychological imperative to dress uniformly and recognizably like others, while responding at the same time to the opposite tug, the impulse to secretly treasure and exhibit occasionally a singular identity or "personality." It is something like "anxiety" that propels both urges: the one toward hiding safely among the mass, thereby avoiding disapproval; the other, the fear of nonentity or insignificance. Which to choose? Or how to balance the equal urges? That is the dilemma undergirding the curious phenomenon of "fashion."

It would seem that Americans more than other people are caught up in this dilemma, and a great deal of our literature and culture owes its existence to this fact. In addition to being America's greatest poet, Walt Whitman was a profound psychologist and social critic. One of his obsessions was the relation between the "simple, separate person" and those "en masse." He was acutely aware of the tension between the American "aristocratic" desire to be singular, if lonely, and the "democratic" urge to seek social safety in numbers. One of his ways of registering this dualism was to advert frequently to the relation of the shore to the sea, the difference between the separate particles of sand and the wholeness of the water. Here, he was exercising himself in a clearly American version of the image of the encounter, and sometimes the reconciliation, of opposites, which kept many thoughtful people awake during the nineteenth century.

Americans are so caught up in their conviction that they enjoy an extraordinary degree of freedom — perhaps encouraged in this belief by every coin's bearing the word "Liberty" — that it is left to foreign visitors to perceive the truth. Here is the British journalist Martin Kettle's observation, published in the *Washington Post:* "Americans tend to think of themselves as a disobedient and not particularly law-abiding nation. Their self-image is of a free life lived at a distance from the law. However, to anyone who lives here for any length of time, that claim often appears strange. The U.S. is a land dominated by social conformity, to say nothing of strictness in the obedience to rules."

There you have it: in one direction, pride at resisting outside pressure. In the opposite direction, nervousness lest one's "freedom" solicit disapproval. The imagination is always proposing images of colorful tights, while the conscience recoils into adhesion to mass styles. And so the safe uniformity of normal life, which supplies so much of value and at the same time cuts off a great deal of what the rest of the world treasures.

Keepsakes

Kay Summersby, Eisenhower's uniformed driver during the Second World War who developed a passion for her boss, had a sense for clothing that combined the normal feminine interest with the unique military attention.

Once, Eisenhower gave Summersby a special gift, a set of tailor-made uniforms like her boss's. In London, the word "tailor" denotes an impressive professional, almost an artist, devoted to making suits expected to last a lifetime. "Every morning," writes Summersby, "when I put on the uniforms I used to feel loved" (by Ike, obviously, but also by the army staff, the group that allowed her to belong and, by doing so, ratified her value). In 1975, in her book *Past Forgetting,* she writes, of those precious uniforms, "I still have one of them. . . . After the war I had it cleaned by the best cleaner in Washington; then I put it away in camphor. It is in one of the packing cases that have followed me here and there for close on thirty years."

Saving one's uniform, or bits of it, for a lifetime, when one's war, which once gave the cloth portentous meaning, is way back in history, is by no means so singular, or perhaps neurotic, an action, as it might seem. Here is Anthony Powell, again revealing his deep interest in details of military uniform. In his novel *The Soldier's Art* (1966), he depicted his autobiographical social noticer Nicholas Jenkins observing the uniform of a

"dugout," an officer young in the First World War called back
into service as a fifty-year-old major for duty in the Second:

> Cap, tunic, trousers . . . all battered and threadbare . . .
> had obviously served him well in the previous war. Frayed
> and shiny with age, they were far from making him look
> down-at-heel in an inadmissible way, their antiquity ac-
> cording a patina of impoverished nobility . . . a gallant dis-
> regard for material things. His Sam Browne belt was limp
> with immemorial polishing.

That resonates with a special British sense of continuity and
sensitivity to the precious reality of the past. But Americans are
not immune to a quasi-mystical, quasi-elegiac, but surely irra-
tional devotion to their uniforms of ages ago. A prime example
was Harry Truman, who, like many veterans, was unable to say
a final goodbye to his military uniforms of the First World War
and, subsequently, of the National Guard. He kept them carefully stored in a footlocker in his attic. My late father, a second
lieutenant of ordnance in the First World War, did exactly the
same — the footlocker, the attic — and his inexplicable keepsakes included even his helmet and gas mask. What were these
two doing, this president and this lawyer? Were they prudently
providing for the possibility of another World War breaking
out soon and their being called up to do their bit again? This
time with a saving in uniform expenses?

In the First World War, Truman was a lieutenant of artillery,
first in the Missouri National Guard, later in the American Ex-
peditionary Force, where, promoted to captain, he commanded
a battery. The war over, he remained in the Army Reserve,
where by 1920 he had achieved the rank of major and, by 1926,
lieutenant colonel, finally retiring as a colonel.

Visitors to the Truman Library near Independence, Missouri, may see a special closet, about ten feet long, designed to
hold HST's numerous uniforms, saved for a lifetime of —
what? Nostalgia? Prudence? Superstition? General unreason?
With a similar totemic instinct for forty years, despite my general detestation of the Army, I carefully saved a group of my

uniform caps from the Second World War, some with the light blue piping designating "Infantry," some with black-and-gold junior officer's piping. After carefully moving them from house to house over the years, I threw them away only in the 1980s.

Is there a similarity between brides and their gowns and soldiers and their uniforms? Certainly. Each carefully saves this evidence of moments when they were younger, more slender and energetic, more hopeful, better looking, and probably of more consequence than now. These keepsakes point to one's past when things made a simple sort of Manichaean sense, well before the arthritis and regrets began to set in.

David McCullough, Truman's biographer, says of these meticulously saved uniforms, "There's something very touching about carefully saved uniforms, and when I saw those at the Truman Library it seemed to me they had their own kind of eloquence." And, I'd add, mystery.

Notes Toward the Reader's

Own Theory of Uniforms

The Uniform Century

It is hard to think of any other man-made object, much less any other garment, that is as physically charged, socially encoded and historically emblematic as the uniform, especially after a century that has seen as much violence and social upheaval as the one just past. Uniforms have long defined tribes, nations, cults and subcultures, divided good guys from bad. They tell us whom to obey, fear, or kill; whom to speak to or ignore; they indicate whom to ask for directions or the check, even whom to ask out.

— *Roberta Smith, a fashion journalist*

Erotica and Related Matters

Uniforms have such mysterious effects on both wearers and audiences that the subject deserves fuller inquiry. And the point is true for both military and civilian uniforms. Certainly the tight fit of military uniforms suggests both the trim figure underneath and the restraint necessary to hold it in good order. The pulp-fiction writer Barbara Cartland, proud of her lifetime attention to the sexual purity of her romance heroines, once said that her notion of a truly sexy man was one "fully clothed and preferably in uniform." (Is it the illusion of broad shoulders and the tight fit that does the job?) And Mae West was quoted as uttering this bit of dialogue: "I always did like a man in uniform. And that one fits you grand. Why don't you come up and see me sometime?"

Victorian pederasts as well as contemporary ones have been found fond of soliciting soldiers and sailors, and it is worth recalling that the lonely British novelist E. M. Forster fell in lifetime love with a uniformed police constable. The Village People, a popular singing group of the 1970s, exploited and at the same time satirized the appeal of uniforms to a homoerotic audience. When they sang sexy numbers like "In the Navy," "Macho Man," and "YMCA," one performer was uniformed as a sailor, another as a policeman, and others as a motorcycle tough, a soldier in battle dress uniform, a cowboy, a construction worker, and an American Indian. A rumor, probably true, holds that recruiters for the Navy actually considered employing the song "In the Navy" in their publicity and advertising, innocent of its homosexual meaning.

Uniforms exert a powerful attraction on lesbians, too. That, at least, is the burden of Linnea Due's book *Uniformsex,* a collection of erotic narratives. Some, of course, are standard items about naughty nurses, but Girl Scouts and high school band members also get a look-in, as do a Federal Express delivery maiden and a girl with a crush on a uniformed waitress. Jessica Gillece concluded an Internet review of Due's book this way: "*Uniformsex* delivers plenty for the connoisseur of erotic fiction, scorching sex, and crisp uniforms. . . . There's plenty to enjoy — and you will never look at your McDonald's server in the same way again."

Vanessa Feitz, writing in the June 1995 issue of *Redbook,*

made an unusual contribution to the sexual psychology of the uniform:

> I married a doctor. I could say I was ensnared by his bed-side manner and blue eyes, but I'd be lying. It was the un-believably erotic combination of stethoscope and clinical coat that won me. . . . A uniform elevates the wearer to a higher plane. . . . In uniform a man is not an individual with weaknesses, annoying habits, and indigestion — he's an ideal.
>
> Marines on parade, marching purposefully while mak-ing our safety their business, are bound to go straight to our hearts. That their thighs look irresistibly taut in their just-pressed pants is gravy. Since we surrender our safety to the skill and courage of these guys, we just can't help imagining surrendering ourselves to them sexually.

And "the hunky UPS man"?

> Lovestruck catalog shoppers confess to making extra purchases just to earn another visit from their UPS driver. Walter Green, a newspaper editor in New York, says he can always tell when the UPS man has arrived. When you hear all the women in the office giggling, you know it's UPS time. They giggle about his body, and they talk about what they want to do in the back of his truck.

Dr. Jeffrey Sonnenfeld, a professor of career studies at Emory University, observed that the UPS uniforms "are flat-tering. They fit nicely around the thigh and they aren't silly or trendy like those harsh blue pleats on the FedEx guys" — one of whom said that in his uniform, with the large-lettered logo, "he looks like a poster."

STUDENTS OF MALE dress, as well as amateur sexologists, will be interested in the current appeal, implicitly sexual, of the military-style touches in nonmilitary clothing. Ginia Bellafante, reporting in the *New York Times* on male fashion shows in Milan in 2001, says, "By the time the men's shows ended . . . editors and buyers had witnessed more leather lace-up boots, Eisenhower jackets, and belted trench coats than if they had stayed home and spent five days with the history channel." And actual military garments are wildly popular among "collectors." One of them reports that "they make you feel macho." *Saving Private Ryan* exerted a powerful influence, making Kaufman's Army and Navy Store, "which occupies a grim patch of West 42nd Street . . . a favorite haunt of stylists as well as construction workers."

But not all the lust for the uniform-like can be traced to sexual impulses. One well-known furnisher of genuine military garments is Juan Gonzalez, who made the uniforms for Spielberg's film. He operates a mail-order business in World War II reproductions. "Among his customers," writes Ms. Bellafante, "he has had veterans who want to be buried in reproductions of their uniforms," in, of course, mainly extra-large sizes now.

After analyzing this fad for uniforms, she concluded that, during the last half-century, "the way military clothes have permeated the popular culture has followed a trajectory from necessity, to rebellion, to reverence." That is, from veterans of the wars wearing out their final uniforms, to anti–Vietnam War protesters, to sentimentalists, with the usual mixture of harmless weirdos.

And, curiously, the garb of the best-known commercial parcel deliverers is equally sought after by those who have no official right to wear it, and from whom it is carefully guarded for security reasons. Robert Frank, in the *Cosmopolitan* article, writes that "UPS caps are selling for $18." And despite the companies' care that their uniforms don't enter the marketplace, leakages occur. "I got a great FedEx jacket from my brother when he quit," says Christopher Lorey, who runs a clothing shop in Atlanta. How did he acquire it? "He just kind of never gave it back," Mr. Lorey explains.

Military Nostalgia

Stefano Tonchi, a men's clothing expert, notes that "the post-modern era has witnessed the proliferation of camouflage prints, cargo pants and backpacks, indicative of the sensation that war is remote and, paradoxically, nostalgia for more heroic days." The irony is that "conflicts and dangers seem to be rapidly finding their way from war zones to our cities. The modern city has become a battlefield, a trench, a society of continuous risk." The comedy is that camouflage garments have become totems of the desirable. The latest emanation is the camouflage mini-bikini vended by Burberry, with extravagant minimal brassiere cups, selling for $115.00.

An Antidote to Loneliness

Someone said, quite correctly, "Loneliness is the one thing no one lies about." And, in severe cases, a uniform seems the only available antidote.

Anomaly

The military is a showcase of anomalies, as might be expected in a "profession" — its word — devoted, in the long run, to killing other people, and not feeling much distress about it.

One of its anomalies is so familiar now as generally to escape notice. In defiance of logic, or even normal monetary values, silver insignia outranks gold. A major has a "gold" leaf, and he is outranked by a lieutenant colonel, wearing a mere silver one. Obviously it should be the other way, but that would be rational or, at least, tending toward good sense.

◀▶

The Case of the Solar Topee

One honorific and generally obsolete piece of uniform is the white solar topee, the tropical hat, usually made of cork or pith covered with white cotton, worn by the ruling class when commanding the dark-skinned locals in India, Burma, the Dutch colonies, and other Asian places managed by Europeans before the Second World War. To disguise its true purpose as part of a uniform of social superiority, the solar topee was given a medical rationalization: the heads of white people, it was said, were special and precious, susceptible, unlike native heads, to damage from strong, direct sunlight.

As George Orwell discovered, "The whole thing was bunkum. . . . Why should the British in India have built up this superstition about sunstroke? Because an endless emphasis on the differences between the 'natives' and yourself is one of the necessary props of imperialism. You can only rule over a subject race, especially when you are in a small minority, if you honestly believe yourself to be racially superior, and it helps towards this if you can believe that the subject race is biologically different," in this case, with skulls so thick and coarse that sunstroke posed for them no danger.

◀▶

The Lancers O the Lancers they're grand

It is often tempting to feel with Henry James that imaginative life in America is somewhat impoverished compared with European possibilities. That suspicion might strike a reader of

Joyce's *Ulysses,* where sometimes the unique uniforms of certain British regiments are noted in all their variety and color. It is hard, then, not to regret the American practice of dressing its whole army in one uniform, without regard to unit differences.

Leopold Bloom is depicted as highly conscious of the complexities of British regimental uniforms, because his late father-in-law, Brian Cooper Tweedy, was a major in the Royal Dublin Fusiliers. Bloom recalls his image in his regimentals, wearing "bearskin cap with hackle plume and accoutrements, with epaulettes, gilt chevrons and sabretaches, his breast bright with medals."

Stopping at a post office, Bloom finds his attention arrested by a "recruiting poster with soldiers of all arms on parade." At first he can't find "old Tweedy's regiment," then thinks he's found the "bearskin cap and hackle plume." But, "no, he's a grenadier. Pointed cuffs. There he is. Royal Dublin Fusiliers. Redcoats. Too showy. That must be why women go after them."

Near the end of *Ulysses* we learn that before her marriage Molly Bloom had been imaginatively captured by the sight of soldiers in uniform. She recalls especially Lieutenant Stanley G. Gardner, dead of enteric fever in the Boer War. "He was a lovely fellow in khaki and just the right height over me. . . . I love to see a regiment pass in review the first time I saw the Spanish cavalry at La Roque it was lovely . . . or those sham battles on the 15 acres the Black Watch with their kilts in time at the march past the 10th Hussars the Prince of Wales Own or the Lancers O the Lancers they're grand or the Dublins that won Tugela."

As we have always suspected, and as the United Parcel Service learned, the best audience for men in uniform is women.

Trade Uniforms

There are some things properly called trade uniforms. Many are now becoming archaic, like the square folded cap made daily from yesterday's newspaper, once de rigueur in press rooms. It was doubtless devised to keep ink out of the printer's hair, but with the advent of cold type and digital proceedings, it is today useless and seldom seen. That is a pity, for it bolstered a worker's pride and added to the mystique of the trade. Another vanished trade uniform, once indispensable, was the tough leather-shoulder semi-jacket worn by the iceman to pad and warm his shoulder when he brought the ice block into the house to install in the icebox. It brought honest pride, too, like the press room cap, for no one else used such a thing for daily work.

Speaking of pride, jockeys traditionally take great pride in their uniforms. Their trade uniform has persisted virtually unchanged for some three centuries. The jockey wears white breeches, black leather boots with three-inch brown leather tops, and the shirt and cap of his employer's colors. The whole is referred to as the "silks." There are two modern items: one, seldom noticed, is the safety vest underneath. The other is the safety helmet, worn beneath the cap. If a jockey shows up for a race without proper uniform, the race course's clerk of scales will prohibit him from competing.

Wartime Uniforms for Everything

During times of war, the term "uniform" becomes so familiar, and carries, curiously, such desirable associations, that it can be invoked for numerous nonmartial purposes that have little to do with the obligatory dress of disciplined groups. For example, during World War II, the makers of one cigarette changed the dominant color of its package from dark green to white. Their advertisement said: "Lucky Strike Green has gone to war! So here's the smart new uniform for fine tobacco."

Uniforms vs. Costumes

A constant problem facing anyone dealing with this subject, and a matter dealt with occasionally in this book, is uniforms vs. costumes. The index of a recently published book contains this item: "Uniforms, *see* Fashion." Highly misleading, for obviously fashions change rapidly (the whole point), while uniforms are more fixed, stable, and continuous. Uniforms indicate respect for the mystery of a usually worthy group and the sense of group loyalty. Wearing a uniform implies pride in being a member. Although the uniforms of the Ku Klux Klan imply the pride of belonging, their main function is to disguise the wearers.

A simple definition of "uniforms" would begin with the idea of obligatory clothing, pleasing to a boss or superior and identical with clothing worn by others in a group. The idea of "group" is essential. The fig leaves worn by Adam and Eve after the Fall are close to costumes, but uniforms are more like the white robes traditionally worn by God and the angels, a boss and a loyal group, together with a concern, almost always present with uniforms, for the general welfare.

There was one occasion in the Second World War when it might be said that fashion made inroads into the world of uniforms. That was when the U.S. Army welcomed the color of officers' "pink" trousers, which went well with the dark green-brown blouse. But that was only for dress uniforms, worn on occasions suggestive more of Hollywood than the brutalities and blood of fighting.

◀▶

On the Level

If you hear two men conversing and making excessive use of phrases like *on the level* or *on the square,* you may be overhearing a Masonic conversation.

The Masonic "uniform" is not really that, for it shows itself too seldom in public, and it is never a complete regulated dress. It is most likely to be seen at Masonic funerals, where the men wear the "aprons" and some of the men wear white gloves and, rarely now, top hats. The Masonic apron is about a foot square, often made of significantly decorated wool, and usually worn over a business suit. It is more a badge than a uniform, like the "jewels" worn on a chain around the neck at lodge meetings, not real jewels but gold or silver ornaments indicating the wearer's office in the local lodge like the pair of keys worn by the treasurer.

No doubt the Masons are a decent lot, but the things they put on can't qualify as uniforms. Too private.

◀▶

A Twentieth-Century Vanity Fair

Alvin Kernan, later a professor of English at Princeton, remembers being an innocent eighteen-year-old on his first liberty from naval boot camp in 1941. He managed to get to San Diego wearing his unexciting white apprentice seaman's "boot's" uniform, embarrassingly devoid of any indications of rank or achievement. In his memoir *Crossing the Line,* his account of his awareness of being among more significant uniforms is a masterpiece, for he never says he is ashamed to be junior and insignificant. The color and action around him do the job.

Of all the walkers on the street, only the boots with floppy white issue uniforms and broad white hats sitting squarely on the head and flaring straight out, neckerchiefs tied at the vee of the jumper rather than at the throat, looked like the real rubes. Everyone else looked in the know, tight uniforms, campaign ribbons, old chief boatswains' mates from the Asiatic station, and long-term hands with rows of gold hash marks. It was an enlisted man's world on the streets. . . .

There was real vulgar joy among so much life. An entire symbology of hierarchy and skill, avidly and quickly learned, flashed along the streets. A red stripe around the left shoulder for below-deck firemen, white around the right for seamen deckhands. Petty officers with ratings badges on the left arm for the trades, on the right for those who worked on deck like quartermasters, gunners, and coxswains. Red hash marks on the lower arm, one for every four years of service; gold hash marks after twenty years. White uniforms, dress blues, khakis and greens here and there on the aviation chiefs.

A genuine twentieth-century Vanity Fair.

Hazards

Military uniforms have this in common with firearms: they are not to be played with.

In the Second World War one RAF unit moved into a new advanced airfield in France. A British pilot walked into an abandoned enemy strongpoint and found some discarded German uniforms. To impress his friends, he put on one of the uniforms and shouted to them as he stepped out of the pillbox.

He was shot stone dead.

It's doubtful that Gunther Billing, Wilhelm Schmidt, and Manfred Pernass, German soldiers in the Second World War, were told, when they donned American uniforms to create confusion behind the American lines, that if they were captured, they would be shot out of hand as spies. They were captured, and they were dealt with by firing squad.

It was the uniforms that did it.

In the American Civil War the industrial North's capacity to manufacture uniforms so far outstripped the South's that its shipments were sometimes highjacked. The Confederates tried to bleach out the blue dye but with little success, and the result was battles with blue-clad forces facing each other. In addition, some soldiers of the South were executed as spies because they were wearing blue uniforms.

◀▶

On Military Influence

The clothing theorist Nick Sullivan has this to say about the way military uniform styles have influenced normal men's dress:

> We may like to think that the military and the civilian are distinct worlds. . . . But in men's fashion the military is there all the time. . . . Throughout the twentieth century, war and its aftermath provided almost all the impetus in the transformation of male style from the fundamentally formal to the fundamentally casual. . . . In World War II, the casual demeanor of American troops serving with Allied forces was a regular source of irritation to their hidebound opposite numbers (and a delight to bored British women).

That is, as a result of the loose, highly informal uniforms the Americans wore to fight in — like, say, the field jacket — loose and informal have ousted trim fit and exaggerated shoulders.

Do Uniforms Enslave?

Alison Lurie, in her book on clothes, at one point may have gone too far in positing a loss of verbal and behavioral freedom among wearers of uniforms. "To put on such livery," she writes, "is to give up one's right to act as an individual." That may sound plausible, and it is certainly politically correct, but it's too simple. To uniform wearers, the language, tone, and gestures of irony and disbelief are always available and often employed. Irony is especially a tool among long-service non-commissioned military officers, as Kingsley Amis was fond of showing in his novels. Irony offers a way of being insolent to officers without giving provable and punishable offense.

"Are you waiting to see me, Sergeant Major?"

"No, sir, I'm just standing here for a bet."

Actually, military uniform allows one to be quite an individual: it can conceal fear, just as it can exaggerate eccentricities. A uniform says a great deal that you don't have to say yourself, and, indeed, one of its functions is to let you assume a character not your own. Sentimental imputations of sincerity are wide of the mark.

Anyone in uniform who can't be sarcastic to the boss without incurring punishment probably lacks the wit, courage, and stamina to be employed at all.

Jacket Vents and Blazers

The British influence on men's uniforms, both military and civilian, should never be underestimated. The single or double vent on a man's jacket has a military origin. It assumes that the wearer, being, of course, an officer and a gentleman, will be mounted most of the time, and the vent keeps the jacket from bunching up when the officer is in the saddle, where he ought to be.

The dark blue blazer, extremely popular with all men, soldiers on leave or not, comes equipped with brass buttons and a thoroughly false narrative of its origins. It is said to have originated aboard the British vessel *Blazer,* some time in the 1860s. The captain of the ship, annoyed at the sloppiness of the crew, ordered them all to wear dark blue serge jackets with brass buttons. Said one retailer of this fancy, "They were uniformly dressed, so that their appearance, and one would assume their behavior as well, was markedly improved."

Rubbish. The blazer is so called because the first ones, worn by members of a crew at the University of Cambridge, were bright red, suggesting the color of fire.

Economics

Although one wouldn't go so far as to assert that wars are started and continued by manufacturers of uniforms, it is clear that, in addition to enriching such industries as aviation, shipping, and munitions, war is a boon to men's clothing manufacturers, as it is to providers of metal insignia, chevrons, divisional patches, leather-visored caps, leather belts, and brown and black footwear.

Before you get into a war, it's best to be certain of your uniform supply — and resupply.

War Correspondents or . . . ?

Because their best-known context is male physical violence, uniforms have usually referred only to the male body and to male duties. Women have been seriously shortchanged. An example: when the first female news correspondents arrived in London in 1942 to send home accounts of the Americans bombing Germany and preparing for the invasion of Europe, no uniforms had yet been designed for them. The very idea of women serving as war correspondents and requiring uniforms was still too novel. And in London especially, clothing was important. The military tailors came forward generously in making uniforms for them: officers' dress jackets (extra room at bust and hips) and skirts made of the officers' gray-pink material. Very nice-looking. But to distinguish the women from real officers, they also wore a green armband with the large letters WC — War Correspondent. It's probable that if every detail of these uniforms had undergone the rigorous attention earned by the male officers' turnout, someone might have noticed the unconscious comedy of the WC. The laughter at this oversight was loud and cruel, finally suggesting to its witless originators that it should be changed. It was, to a harmless letter C.

Prostitutes Don Uniforms for Work

Mexico City (Reuters), May 16, 2001

Prostitutes in Mexico's Caribbean resort city of Cancun are going the way of soldiers, police, and soccer players by donning uniforms for their work. About 50 prostitutes began using the uniforms — tight black shorts and yellow tops — while working Cancun's streets and bars over the weekend.

Insignia and Shame

If you were an enlisted serviceman in the 1940s, you'd have wanted to proclaim your manhood by being assigned to the right kind of work. It was easier to conceal what sort of work that was in the Army than in the Navy. In the Army, you'd wear on your sleeve a chevron of your rank (corporal or sergeant) with a letter T underneath it, signaling that you were a technician and not a fighting person. If you were, say, a chaplain's assistant, a job widely scorned because it was, lots of people thought, held by effeminates and jerks, you wore the same T/5 chevron as a highly regarded ordnance specialist working with high explosives or adjusting the pull on rifle triggers, and thus contributing something manly to the war effort. As a T/5, you could pass for something not entirely contemptible.

But in the Navy, your sissy work would be blazoned on your sleeve for all to see and condescend to. You were marked indelibly as a bugle master, a storekeeper, a radio technician, a carpenter's mate, or an officers' cook. Everyone was privy to the terrible truth about you; you were not a real salt, only a prudent civilian dressed up, the next thing to a draft dodger.

Shoulder Knots

"You are judged by your luggage," said an advertisement in the 1980s. In the eighteenth and nineteenth centuries, a handy device in comic and even philosophic writing was to insist ironically that human beings are actually made by their tailors and dressmakers. In *A Tale of a Tub*, in 1704, Jonathan Swift imagined a silly person pointing and shouting, "That fellow has no soul; where is his shoulder knot?" A century later, Thomas Carlyle had fun with the same device, pretending that he believed in the identity of man and clothing. And a century after that, Virginia Woolf, as we have seen, affected to mistake the academic uniform for the wearer. "This man is a very clever man," because he wears the gown and hood of a doctor of letters.

All very funny, and yet it is an implicit assumption in armies and navies and universities that the wearer of a uniform *becomes* the person associated with the values it represents, and thus increases in courage, obedience, loyalty, and intellect by the act of putting on the livery of the boss.

A Canadian Airman, in London, 1941

Nights were spent going from pub to pub, chatting up the WAAF's or WREN's or WAAC's or the Land Army girls. Of all the uniforms worn by the girls, the Land Army Girl's uniform was the hardest to remove. Heavy, dark green turtleneck sweater, tucked into breeches, that were tucked into knee-high boots. We called them the "iron maidens."

Bagpipers' Dress

On St. Patrick's Day especially, Irish rather than Scottish bagpipers are to be seen and heard. And since their different uniforms are traditional and invariable, it might seem that they are in competition and dislike each other. But no.

Tom Downes, a well-known bagpiper in New York, declares that there is not and never has been any bad blood between the two groups. They don't perform together, and each has a special audience, but that's all. Their uniforms are different, but only an expert could detect all the differences. Irish pipers traditionally wear a kilt of solid color instead of the Scottish plaid. They wear a short jacket and a tenue more sedate than the Scots' outfit, which may feature military caps, ribbons, and epaulets. While most Scottish pipers wear the military Glengarry cap, the Irish wear a civilian beret. It can be said that the Irish pipers wear a demilitarized version of the Scottish uniform, and that the rejected Scottish touches reflect Irish annoyance at the long British occupation of Ireland. But if there is public resentment elsewhere, it's not felt by Irish pipers, at least when they're in uniform. They have doubtless lifted many a glass to the health of their Scottish counterparts.

Mark Twain on Men's Civilian Uniform

Like D. H. Lawrence, Mark Twain found the conventional man's dark suit, worn for business and the Senate, tedious and offensive. In December 1905 Mark Twain went to Washington to give his views on copyright law. He wore a white suit, which occasioned some criticism. In defense, he said that he preferred brilliant startling colors to "the dark and somber clothes men usually wore and which had a melancholy and depressing effect on him." He went on to indicate a preference for "the clothes of the Middle Ages, which were resplendent with colors, plumes, and trappings of a brilliant hue." He added, "Whenever I go to a theatre and see a lot of men rigged out in that abomination of all clothing, a dress suit, they remind me of a flock of crows. . . . There is no reason why men should not wear brighter colored clothing, especially in these dark winter months." Unlike Lawrence, Mark Twain wore the odd clothes he admired, observing, "When a man gets to be seventy-one years old, as I am, he can wear the clothes he likes best."

"They Found a Home in the Army"

That was the way intelligent browned-off conscripts during the Second World War described those who seemed to glory in being ordered about and treated with programmatic contempt by twenty-year-old lieutenants, as well as relishing crappy Army food and lapping up the mental regimentation. And, of course, wearing the awful dirt-colored uniform. Such soldiers were regarded with mingled pity and disdain by the skeptical and the disgusted.

Many of those pitiable creatures, upon their return to civilian life, joined the American Legion, which provided a sentimental afterglow of military practices, such as saluting, coming to attention, and enjoying pseudo-military titles and jargon, like "post" for the name of the local branch, and "Commander" for its president. It was almost like the joy of still being in the Army. Not the least of the legion's attractions for such people was its formal uniform, worn on public memorial occasions, where the presence of the legion was required for color-guarding, recitation of the names of the fallen, and similar patriotic observances. Recalling the Army dress uniform, the present legion version is in some ways an improvement, not least in its color, dark blue (the naval influence yet again). The jacket has four buttoned flap-pockets, four brass buttons down the front, a stripe around each cuff, and the legion emblem and post number on each lapel. As in the Army, medal ribbons may be worn above the left pocket. White shirt and black tie suggest heightened social standing and seriousness, although the preposterous "overseas" cap may spoil the effect a bit. But it is doubtless unfair to ridicule an institution whose beer brings pleasure to so many.